THERE FOR THE TAKING

JAMES N. WHIDDON
WITH LANCE ALSTON

TRUE BETA PUBLISHERS

A True Beta Publishers Publication

Editor: Cindie Geddes
Page design: Megan Hughes, Eh? Clerical Services Inc.
Cover design: Synerjet Studios

Printed in the United States of America
10 9 8 7 6 5 4 3 2 1

ISBN No. 0-9758572-0-7

Dedication

To my beloved wife Elizabeth
Who chose to invest her life with mine.

And

To my sons Johnathan and Daniel
Who have brought me immeasurable wealth.

Contents

PART 1: WALL STREET'S FAILED METHODS

1   Chapter
Market Timing   **15**

2 Chapter
Stock Picking   *31*

3 Chapter
Chasing Returns   *53*

4 **Chapter**

The Financial Services Industry 67

PART II: WEALTH WITHOUT WORRY

5 **Chapter**

The Answer is Right in Front of You 81

CONTENTS

Preface

Two hundred and twenty-seven years ago, Thomas Jefferson wrote the following in the American Declaration of Independence:

"A Prince whose character is thus marked by every act which may define a Tyrant, is unfit to be the ruler of a free people."

Just as the truths of America's greatest document were held to be self-evident, we believe that all investors have the right to benefit from free capital markets. Those that now "rule" Wall Street must be exposed for what they are – tyrants.

Whenever the leaders of capital market institutions harm those for whom they exist to help, their power must be removed. When a prolonged record of abuses is evident, their methods must be exposed. When malfeasance and misleading information become overbearing, it is the right of each participant to demand fair treatment. It is time for a change.

When we ponder the historical figures who championed free capital markets, we see leaders with revolutionary ideas – *revolution* as defined as "a drastic and far-reaching change in ways of thinking and behaving." We don't use this word casually, but there is no better word to accurately describe the ideas we wish to convey in this book.

Capital markets were created for the benefit of those who participate in them. Over time, Wall Street autocrats have usurped our rights as investors.

The playing field must be leveled. It is time for *every* individual investor to learn the truth about how they can triumph in the investing arena. There should be *no losers*. Investing is not a zero-sum game. Free capital markets make it possible for *everyone* to win. Yes, that means *everyone* can have a piece of an ever-expanding pie. *Free markets work.*

In the end, you will realize that the important questions concerning investing have been answered. As a blessed participant in the greatest economic system in the history of mankind, it is time for you to prosper. It is time to create wealth without worry, which is truly *there for the taking*.

I

Introduction

What Wall Street says and does and where Wall Street leads, most investors blindly follow. This book is not for those followers. This book is for investors who have always suspected that Wall Street is only interested in promoting a system that benefits Wall Street first. Any benefit to individual investors is secondary.

This book is written for those who are frustrated with the constant barrage of confusing and conflicting investment information, hit and miss approaches and exaggerated return claims. *There for the Taking* is written for those who are tired of having the worries of their financial *future* rob them of their life's *present*. This book is for all who ever thought the odds were stacked against them in the investing game. This book will change all that.

While this book is intended to be read in sequential order as a case is built *against* the status quo and *for* free market investing, it can be a valuable reference guide as well.

In the first half of the book, Wall Street's popular methods used in portfolio management and the current delivery system of financial services is explored. Most investment strategies focus on improving returns through market *timing* and stock *picking*. These techniques are otherwise known as *active management*. Yet if these practices are so effective, why have the returns for the overwhelming majority of investors lagged well behind the market indices?

The first two chapters will outline the reasons that active management is by and large a futile exercise efficient only to the degree that it lines the pockets of Wall Street executives and brokers. For the first time, you will understand why these failed methodologies are well aligned with Wall Street's interests, but are *mis*aligned with the interests of individual investors.

Chapter 3 will examine the endemic tendency of most investors – *chasing returns*. Return chasing is, of course, a direct result of subscribing to the idea that investors can successfully time and pick the market. The research reveals that investors consistently arrive at the party late. The returns they seek have already occurred. The discussion will show how chasing higher returns causes investors to buy high and sell low and how this typically results in netting less than *half* the market index returns.

Chapter 4 takes a look at the financial services industry and the situation as it currently exists at the *user* level. In other words, at the system's point of entry – the investment advisor. Most consumers seeking investment advice find it difficult to determine the difference between one financial service professional and another. It is important to define what type of advisor to use and what an advisor should and should not do when servicing a client.

The second half of the book is designed to be the *solutions* section. For the first several years of my financial services career, I too was caught up in the failed Wall Street system that seeks to use the active management techniques of timing and picking to reach investment goals. Fortunately, I was quickly enlightened to the logic of *market return* investing and its obvious advantages. Since this epiphany, I have made it my goal to rescue as many investors as would listen to the story.

Chapter 5 offers time-tested data that will prove conclusively that market returns are indeed *there for the taking*. This discussion is designed to give you faith in the miracle of capitalism rather than in human soothsaying. *All* investors can have a long-term successful investing experience by *not* succumbing to the Wall Street shell games.

Chapter 6 is intended to put the finishing touches on your understanding of what it takes to achieve proper portfolio management for the ages. It is designed to give an overview of how to properly arrange a portfolio. Specifics concerning the construction of the *Market Return Portfolio™* will be detailed. This will include information on diversification and a discussion of asset allocation and its merits. Finally, exactly which investment vehicles to use will round out the discussion. This includes the one alternative we believe is best.

Once you have fully digested this book, it will become apparent just how market returns can be harnessed in a simple, consistent fashion. You will have a map to investing success and understand that the answer does not lie in some new scheme, but rather in an obvious but too often overlooked fiscal reality. The answers have always been there; you will now have what the Wall Street tyrants conceal.

The content of this book will not be widely accepted by the securities industry establishment. After all, what is revealed will not only raise the ire of industry players as their investing methods are attacked, but it also could cost them their jobs. However, my hope is that securities professionals will take a deep introspective look at their own character and integrity and do what is right for their clients.

While some of the general principles discussed may be familiar, you will learn things here that you have never heard before. It is quite likely that a complete paradigm shift will occur as you ponder the processes and evidence presented. You will ask questions such as: "Why haven't I heard this before?" and "Why isn't everyone doing this?" This book offers the answers.

I sincerely believe *There for the Taking* will stimulate you to take a new informed look into the investment arena. In it you will find the answers about your money for which you have been searching. In the end, our hope is to learn that you have found financial *peace of mind* – which is priceless.

PART I:
WALL STREET'S FAILED METHODS

"Such is the irresistible nature of truth that all it asks, and all it wants, is the liberty of appearing."
– Thomas Paine

1 Chapter
Market Timing

Mr. and Mrs. Jones are a very intelligent, well-educated couple who like to think they are pretty good at making important decisions, including those that have a lasting effect on their retirement nest egg. For example, they made an investment decision to get back into the stock market in late 1994, which was just at the bottom of the market cycle they had patiently waited out. In March 2000, the Joneses decided that the bull had run its course, and it was time to get out of the market completely. They did so, to their great advantage, as the markets went into a 31-month dive. In November of 2002, the Joneses decided correctly again and invested all of their money back into the market as the run-up in stock prices began. Until this day, they continue to know just when to get in and out of the market by making intelligent decisions based on *obvious* market data.

Clearly this is a fantasy.

People can't predict the future. We all know this on an intellectual level. So why do so many believe it to be different in the investment world? Because investors so *want* to believe it. If market timing were possible, we wouldn't see the investment accounts of Americans fall by trillions of dollars as they did from March of 2000 to November of 2002 during the worst bear market since The Great Depression.

Market timing is a cornerstone of an ineffective philosophy known as *active portfolio management*. The word *active* is often misconstrued as having a positive connotation. After all, investors expect their brokers to do *something*. They certainly do not want them to sit around and do *nothing*.

Being active implies that brokers are indeed doing something to make positive things happen in the portfolios that are under their supervision. As we will soon see, however, the *more* active a broker is with an account, the *less* likely positive things will occur.

The idea that markets can be timed successfully is perhaps the easiest investing untruth to lay bare. Many investors and brokers say they know when to get in or out of the market. At some point they must come to the realization that they do not and *cannot* know where the markets are going. We humbly admit that we learned this lesson some time ago – but not without making the same mistakes most investors and brokers have made.

We learn at an early age that hindsight is 20/20, yet there is a lingering belief that *we* may be different somehow – a belief that perhaps our makeup allows us to analyze and predict accurately when it comes to securities markets. This behavioral characteristic in the financial world is known as *hindsight bias*: the concept that we can predict future events rationally based on the information we have concerning past events. Yet a disclaimer such as "past performance is no guarantee of future results" is required by law on investment literature and prospectuses. We all know that, absent dumb luck, we must have foreknowledge in order to profit from a race that has yet to be run.

THE MEDIA'S ROLE

Market timing is also a media darling. Nearly every major financial publication and broadcast in the country is based, at least in part, upon the premise that successfully timing the market is a possibility. "Why You Should Own Technology Stocks Now" and "The Coming Market Boom (or Bust)" are common examples of headlines that attract investors like moths to a porch light on a warm summer evening. They promote the belief that timing the market is within the average investor's grasp.

It is not hard to understand why investors make poor decisions when they rely on the daily news for their investment advice. But in all fairness, we do not believe that the financial media is trying to mislead anyone.

Most members of the media are well-intentioned, honest citizens. Their job is to report the news or opinions of the day, not to give financial advice. These are two very different propositions.

The trouble is that most investors misconstrue the news of the day (or random opinions) as advice. This speaks to the tremendous influence the mass media has in our lives. So while the daily news can be interesting and fun to talk about around the water cooler or at the kitchen table, it rarely has a lasting effect on capital markets.

NOTED EXPERTS ON TIMING

Peter Lynch was once quoted as saying: "Attempting to forecast whether the market is at a peak or in a valley – and whether to buy or unload stocks as a result – is a waste of time. I don't know anyone who has been right more than *once in a row*."[1]

Here is a man whom many regard as one of the great investment gurus of our time. We figure that if ever there were a great stock market timer, it was Peter Lynch. Yet he clearly states that the timing game cannot be won. And as you look a little deeper into his statement you see the wisdom of it. In order to time the market successfully, one must indeed be right at least *twice* in a row. You must know when to get in and when to get out or when to get out and when to get back in. If you miss on either decision, you lose.

Another famous investment industry pioneer, John Bogle, founder of the Vanguard Group, said, "In 30 years in the business, I do not know anyone who knows anyone who has done it [timed the market] successfully and consistently. My impression is that trying to do market timing is likely, not only *not* to add value to your investment program, but to be counterproductive."[2]

THE MARKET HATES UNCERTAINTY

There is nothing more fickle than the securities markets. An example of this fickleness and unpredictability came with the days leading up to the war with Iraq in 2003.

On March 13ᵗʰ, news came out that the war with Iraq could be delayed or perhaps even avoided. There were rumors of Iraqi generals wanting to surrender before the first shot was fired. The Dow Jones Industrial Average took off that day by 269.68 points. Four days later, on March 17ᵗʰ, it became obvious that war was imminent and the Dow took off again with another increase of 282.2 points. How could this be? This is an example of how the market doesn't hate war or other calamitous events as much as it hates *uncertainty*. The market looked upon these two opposite developments as positive for stocks because closure on the important war issue was potentially at hand. Go figure.

WIDELY USED TIMING TECHNIQUES

One common tool used to time market sectors and individual securities is *technical analysis*. This involves the making and interpreting of stock charts. (Those who engage in this activity are sometimes called *chartists*.) Technical analysis is something we see quite often in newsletters dedicated to timing. These publications claim charting offers a scientific way to make logical decisions about markets.

In a discussion of technical analysis we might talk about terms such as a *bullish trend*, which is an upward movement in the stock price and thus the charted line as seen here in Figure 1.1.

Figure 1.1
Charting a Bullish Trend

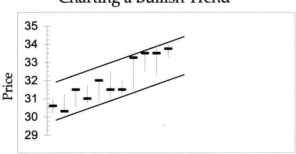

Time

A *bearish trend* would head in the opposite direction. Or perhaps we would hear about the *shoulders* formed from the slight up and down movements that would eventually form a *neckline*. Once the neckline is broken through, it is said to be a *bearish* signal (see Figure 1.2).

Figure 1.2
Charting a Bearish Trend with Shoulders

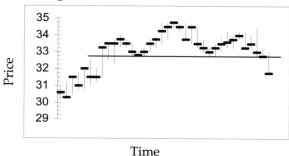

Time

Charting is simply a matter of connecting the dots to find distinguishable patterns of prices on which to make predictions. All of this is designed to bring about a feeling that some detailed work and analysis has taken place.

Such a tracking technique clearly appeals to an investor who is more interested in profits from daily trading vs. long-term investing. But this is a failed system for two reasons:

1. No secrets. If this worked as well as some would argue, then the playground would get very crowded. The buy or sell indicator would be of little value if many others were acting on the same information.

2. Randomness. The chartist relies on his or her ability to read changes in direction or status of a stock price or market. As we'll discuss, the price of a stock is dependent on many random factors that usually occur somewhat rapidly – sometimes *very* rapidly.

Even if charts are coded rigorously into a computer and then tested, they produce no statistical basis for making money; they are simply wishful thinking. The chartist's reliance on the momentum to change before making a trading decision will more times than not leave them standing at the station as the train leaves.

DATA MINING

Data mining is another common technique among market timers. Sometimes called *data snooping*, it is a methodology that can look very much like a credible way of arriving at investment decisions. For example, data miners might consider prevailing interest rates or industrial production in relation to stock market performance over an extended period of time. With many charts, graphs and PhDs at their side, data miners may proceed to make a very compelling case for initiating an important investment move or strategy. However, at their core, data miners are still involved with market timing and have little or no reliable evidence to support a claim that their methods work consistently over the long term.

When it comes to data mining, almost anything can be used to prove a point. If you are a sports fan, you may recall an instance of data mining that was well publicized a few years ago when it was discovered that each time the NFC team defeated the AFC team in the Super Bowl, we could expect an up year in the stock market. Where did this crazy notion come from? Well, for several years the pattern held true and thus someone noted it. Others have referenced hemlines, sunspots or even butter production in Bangladesh as reliable indicators of market direction.

When it comes to data mining, the famous quote from Mark Twain holds true:

> *"Figures often beguile me, particularly when I have the arranging of them myself; in which case the remark attributed to Disraeli would often apply with justice and force: 'There are three kinds of lies: lies, damned lies and statistics.'"*[3]

> — *Autobiography of Mark Twain*

TIMING NEWSLETTERS

Timing newsletters and other publications dedicated to timing are popular among the investing public as individuals try to decide their next investing moves. Evidence suggests that these publications are some of the worst of all possible sources for investment advice. There are hundreds of these timing publications in the United States, ranging from the barely plausible to the absurd. The average monthly subscription cost can range from $100 to $200. The fact that most are published monthly begs the question: "With news changing minute by minute, how timely can *monthly* advice be?"

Timing newsletters are notorious for charting (technical analysis) and data mining. Unfortunately, some of these publications do offer "winning" advice on a random basis. We say "unfortunately" because this occasional correct guess leads the public to believe that the writers are skilled in the art of timing the market. But market timing newsletters, not ironically, get it right about as often as "professional" money managers.

Noted author, analyst and money manager David Dreman did a detailed study tracking opinions of market prognosticators dating back to 1929 and found them to be correct only about 23 percent of the time.[4] A coin flipper would be right 50 percent of the time. Yet the publications continue to thrive as investors somehow think *they are different*.

When a newsletter hits it right, even one time, its authors tend to live on the success for years – perhaps even decades. The trouble is that readers suffer because they put their faith in the publication's information based on one pick, or a short run of successes. (Remember Peter Lynch's quote on being right "more than once in a row"?) Yet what do these proxy advisors really have on the line other than the loss of another subscriber? With so many investors having the lottery mentality of "hitting it big," along with ultra short memories, these timing newsletter publishers will probably always have plenty of revenue.

NO TIMING ADVANTAGE

Figure 1.3 shows three very different investment timing results. Each of the three is supposed to have invested systematically in the Standard and Poor's 500 Index (S&P 500) once per quarter for 30 years ending in 2003.

Loser Lenny tried to time his deposits just right. Unfortunately he bought on the *worst* possible day (highest price) each quarter during the 30-year period. He had perfectly *bad* timing. *Fortunate Fran* bought the same amount on the *best* possible day (lowest price) for the same time period. She had perfectly *good* timing for 120 straight quarters. *Steady Eddie* did not use any timing technique and simply set up an automatic investment program without any regard whatsoever to the market status. In other words, he put the money in on the first day of the quarter and said, "I'll check it in 30 years." The results are striking.

Figure 1.3
S&P 500: Quarterly Investing
1974-2003 Best and Worst Days

Loser Lenny (Buys at High)	**9.1%**
Fortunate Fran (Buys at Low)	**9.6%**
Steady Eddie (1st Day of Quarter)	**9.4%**

Data Source: MSN Money

The fact that over a 30-year period, the difference between a perfectly bad timer and a perfectly good timer is only about half a percent is phenomenal. We can only reason that since there are no perfect timers in either direction – good or bad – that any timing attempts will average out over the long run. That is exactly what happened here.

The message: Don't watch markets or try to time them – just be *in* them.

TIME IN THE MARKET IS EVERYTHING!

Market timing still enjoys great appeal. Yet the case *against* this investing technique grows stronger with each passing day. Recent data shows the utter futility of trying to guess what will happen in the markets.

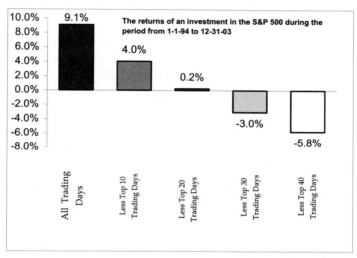

Data Source: MSN Money

This graph shows how missing only a few of the market's best days would have a huge negative effect on the returns of an investment in the S&P 500 Index during this 10-year period. The most dramatic message from the chart is that if you had missed the best 40 days out of the more than 3,600 days of that period (a little over 1 percent), you would have *lost* 5.8 percent per year vs. *gaining* 9.1 percent per year if you had stayed in for the entire time. That is a **14.9 percent** difference! (Please keep in mind this time period represents some of the best *and* worst years in market history.) So given this evidence, why would any prudent investor sit on the sidelines and wave at those still marching in the market parade? The answer is *panic*, pure and simple. Investors see the storm around them (pending war, economic slump, etc.) and take their eyes off the goal and the facts that tell them that staying the course is the only sensible way to proceed. The talking head investment analysts all say something different depending on what bubble they think will burst next. The media unwittingly contributes to the volatile atmosphere by reporting mostly bad news because good news does not sell copies. What do investors think other than the sky is falling? Investors run for cover in cash and fixed income instruments and out of equities because they see bonds as a traditionally "safe" investment vehicle. This will presumably calm their nerves and enable them to *miss* the bad stock market. But this "safety" will be only an illusion and not a reality. Unfortunately, this fact will be learned too late for most.

So what to do? The alternative to market timing is long-term, steadfast investing. Adhering to an *Investment Policy Statement* (IPS) regardless of short-term fluctuations eliminates any guesswork. (An Investment Policy Statement is a written document that defines your objectives and constraints and helps maintain a sound long-term plan, even when short-term market movements cause second-guessing.) Once your IPS is complete, it will:

- define the level of risk with which you are comfortable;
- establish the expected investment time horizon;
- determine the rate of return needed, based on retirement cash flow needs;
- prescribe the asset classes to be used;
- document the investment methodology used in managing your portfolio; and
- help determine the means for making any adjustments to your current portfolio.

Giving way to fear will undermine your investment program. There may be times and circumstances when an adjustment in your asset allocation is needed. But make sure this decision stems from the long-term strategy as outlined in your plan and not from overconfidence in your ability to predict market movements. Whenever you become tense about markets, review the historical data to regain your confidence in your long-term strategy, and remember this simple thought: it is not *timing* the markets, it is *time in* the markets that brings long-term investment success.

LOOKING TO THE EXPERTS

On December 5, 1996, Federal Reserve Chairman Alan Greenspan made his famous "irrational exuberance" speech in which he warned of an overheating market based on inflated valuations and then a subsequent possibility of an "unexpected and prolonged contraction" ala Japan.[5] The S&P 500 Index proceeded to grow for the next 3 ¼ years from 744 to a peak of 1,527 on March 23, 2000.

Greenspan was right about the bubble bursting – only trouble is it was more than three years later. The index then dropped steadily, hitting a low of 776 on October 9, 2002 before it once again changed directions. This 2 ½ year period of market decline was hardly the "Japanotype" contraction of which Greenspan warned.

So how did Alan Greenspan have such poor timing on his prognostication? Is there anyone on earth that has better financial data and resources at their disposal to make forecasts? If Mr. Greenspan does not have the ability, should we believe that there are money managers who can predict market anomalies in such a way as to benefit their clients? And if they did, would they be inclined to share this kind of information?

Figure 1.4

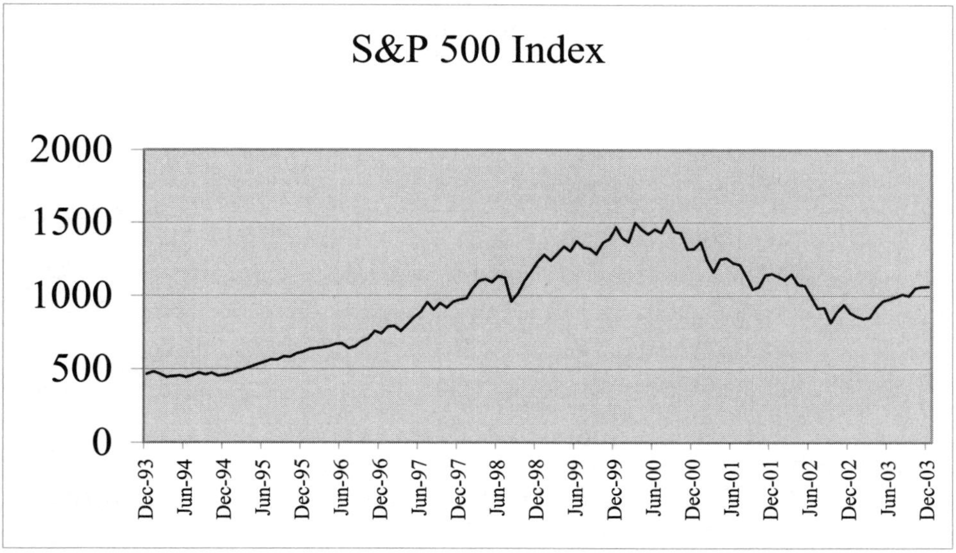

Data Source: MSN Money

Many market timing brokers and newsletter writers have told us that their real value is most apparent in turbulent, fast-moving markets. In the last decade, we have had a perfect laboratory in which to view the performance of "professional" market timing money managers. Figure 1.4 shows a 3+ year bull market and a 2 ½ year decline followed by another 14-month run up. How did the experts fare during this period that was supposedly "perfect for timers"?

- S&P 500 Index average annualized return: **10.97 percent**[6]
- Average annualized return for active United States large cap fund managers: **9.19 percent**[7]
- United States large cap active managers that beat the S&P 500 Index: **23.7 percent**[8]

Clearly there is a limit to any success that can be gleaned from market timing strategies. A related dictum attributed to economist John Maynard Keynes is: "Markets can remain irrational longer than you can remain solvent." In other words, a market timer's best efforts are usually no match for the fickle market.

COPING WITH THE BEAR

In the midst of any bear market, there is that nagging temptation to either sneak out of the markets or engage in an all-out mad dash to the hills, seeking refuge from the storm in the form of bonds or cash equivalents. The question on everyone's mind is: "When will it all end?" Ironically, more often than not, the darker the mood of the masses, the nearer the end we are.

There's certainly no stronger evidence of that mood than in the media's coverage of bear markets. We should be reminded that the news in the investing world is rarely, if ever, all bad – even in the worst of times (such as we experienced from March of 2000 through October of 2002). Investors who implement maximum diversification and ignore timing techniques can actually gain ground in some asset classes during a market downturn. (small U.S. value, for example, gained 16.11 percent as represented by the Russell 2000 value index during the March 2000 to October 2002 time period mentioned). While this may not completely spare investor portfolios from the claw of a bear market, it will most certainly result in a buffering effect allowing most, if not all, long-term financial objectives to remain intact.

In spite of dark economic clouds that appear occasionally, the best time to buy equities is always *now*. As long as the world turns, families grow, children need food, clothing, shelter and education and the entrepreneurial spirit thrives, an economy — and thus the markets — *must* grow.

Owning stocks is the only way to effectively hedge against inflation – and its evil twin, taxation – and create long-term wealth. We know the long-term, after-inflation, after-tax historical return of stocks over bonds is approximately 3 to 1. Regardless of the current emotional climate in the financial markets, those numbers defy argument.

While seeking refuge in bonds or cash may provide some restful nights in the short term, it is (due to opportunity costs) an extremely expensive sleep aid.

The only sure way to miss the tremendous gains that follow a market downturn is to exit the game before it is over. Stay focused on your goals, keep that investment chin up and stay in the market!

WHY MARKET TIMING DOESN'T WORK

We've shown several examples and discussed the failings of market timing as a long-term strategy. The fundamental reason it is impossible to consistently time the market is that the securities markets are *efficient*. Consider the following:

1. Rapid communication. The age in which we live affords instantaneous access to accurate data. This fact supports the idea of how difficult it is to get an "edge" on anyone concerning the receipt of information. Perhaps before the computer age came about, we could learn something about an investment idea that would provide a small window of opportunity for profit. But with the advent of the personal computer, that probability has all but vanished even for the professional.

2. Financial analysts act immediately. Because the information is so readily available, intelligent, qualified professionals are well equipped to act. The problem with this is that any data, no matter how accurate, cannot be acted upon in a timely fashion so as to gain an advantage. Ironically, these analysts are all so good at what they do that they cancel out the efforts of one another. We call this the *efficient analyst paradox*. The more numerous the qualified competitors, the less likely one will achieve greater results.

3. *New* information. The news is inherently unpredictable. One needs only to look at any financial news channel on a weekday to see this exhibited. On the television screen, (usually at the bottom), there is a ticker that changes every three seconds to reflect that this new information has been processed into the market. As a result, the price of any one stock or market reflects all the known information at that moment in time. So to select undervalued stocks at the right time consistently is extremely difficult.

4. Random events. Events that have nothing to do with the intrinsic financial health of companies can dramatically influence their stock prices. We need to go no further than September 11, 2001 to

understand this truth in its purest form. While the airline industry was surely struggling before this horrific event, could they have ever dreamed of, much less controlled, the negative effect it would have? Conversely, companies in the homeland security industry have seen a boon from the unfortunate results of this attack. Other events, such as oil embargos, a SARS epidemic, tax legislation, as well as many others, can also influence stock prices – allowing absolutely no control to analysts or investors.

SUMMARY

In a dynamic capitalist economy, market timing is a fool's errand. By looking closer at the "professional" timing techniques through a common sense lens, we can see that they are simply decoys designed to distract us from this reality. In our discussion, we have learned how the data shows randomness in market fluctuations that cannot be controlled or predicted by mere humans. Furthermore, when faced with the facts surrounding the efficiency of the securities markets and the uncertainty of arbitrary events, logic dictates that timing the market is ineffective. In short, *time in* the market, regardless of market conditions or undulations, will ultimately provide the return and purchasing power protection that an investor needs to succeed.

Chapter

Stock Picking

The second component of active portfolio management is *stock picking*. While there are many brokers and investment managers who would admit that timing the market is a fool's struggle, they almost all still subscribe to the theory that winning stocks can be picked successfully. The fallacy of this assumption is that this means someone else – namely most everyone else (i.e. the market) – must be wrong. We must ask ourselves: What are the chances of that being the case? This entire *picking* concept is nothing more than *speculating*; it is <u>not</u> *investing*.

Speculation involves the idea that you cast your lot with a particular security or sector (such as technology) and then you either win or you lose. There is no middle ground. Now there is nothing wrong with speculation as long as you understand the risks. But do not confuse speculating with investing.

Investing involves understanding the concept that *everyone* can be a winner. Yes, that means *everyone* can have a piece of an ever-expanding pie. *Every* investor can have a successful experience. With capitalism, market returns are essentially *there for the taking*. Investing is *not* a zero-sum game.

SUCCESS FOR ALL

How can we make this claim of "everybody wins"? Easy, we believe in the efficiency of the free market. And we're not alone in our beliefs. Great leaders such as Abraham Lincoln, Theodore Roosevelt and Ronald Reagan all shared our faith in the people and ideals of capitalism and democracy. They knew then just as we know now that *free markets work.*

Capitalism, which promotes the free setting of prices based on the decisions and values of the entire economy, is the reason our current way of life prevails. There are billions of factors at work in the economy at any given time. Individuals and business entities make continuous decisions all affecting the system in different ways – some positive, some negative, some indifferent. But the system works. It is a phenomenon that engenders an indomitable spirit that can be found all over the world. To prove this, one would need only to examine three of the most profound economic experiments of the last 60 years. They are: West Germany vs. East Germany, South Korea vs. North Korea and mainland China vs. Hong Kong. In these examples we see a stark contrast between what government intervention in the form of regulation of prices (both for goods and markets) can do versus what allowing the markets to find their own way in setting prices can do. This lack of intervention (which ultimately drives economic growth) provides opportunities for individuals – and thus capital markets.

Will we still experience difficult markets periodically? Count on it. When? Who knows? And furthermore, who cares? As long as we have the system that allows prices to seek their own way, then economic growth will occur. With this in mind, shouldn't investors be most afraid of *not being* in the market when it goes to 20,000 rather than *being* in the market if it goes down to 2,000? In time, one is *certain* to happen, the other is not.

OPTIMISM – THE ONLY REALITY

During the bear market recession of 2000 through 2002 a luncheon was held with Senior Vice President and Chief Economist for the Federal Reserve Bank of Dallas, Michael Cox. Before he began his speech he indicated that there would be a Q&A session when he finished. He stated, "Before you ask the question, let me just say that the American economy is sound. I am accused often of being an optimist. In fact, I am simply a realist. There has never been a recession that we have *not* come out of, and I do not expect it to be any different this time."

BULLS AND BEARS

To bring this idea into focus, Figure 2.1 below shows the history of United States bull and bear markets based on the S&P 500 Index over a time period of more than seven decades.

Figure 2.1

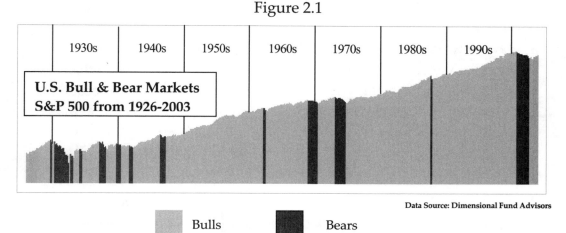

Data Source: Dimensional Fund Advisors

Bulls   Bears

Note the duration of the bull markets vs. the bear markets.[1] In total, bull markets have dominated in the United States more than *80 percent* of the time. The bull runs went *up* a total of 3,684 percent versus going *down* a total of 451 percent during the bear cycles. Furthermore, the average *gain* for the 14 bull market time periods was 263 percent. This compares to an average *loss* of 35 percent for the 13 bear markets. Is it now easier to understand our absolute confidence in capital markets?

This inevitable expansion of capital markets is a windfall for all who are *market return* investors.

A PARADIGM SHIFT

If it is true that capital market returns are truly available for all, then it is imperative that we, as investors, change our way of thinking about our portfolios – including the *size* of our holdings.

For example, if a tax-deferred portfolio (such as an IRA) is worth $1 million today and receives a return of 10 percent, its value will be $10,834,705 in 25 years. Do you not then own a $10 million+ asset and not a $1 million asset if this growth (i.e., *market return*) is there for the taking?

We must concern ourselves with the best possible way to *protect* the *market return* (the $10 million+) that is rightfully ours as fortunate participants in the great capitalist system we have inherited. Furthermore, as good stewards, are we not *obligated* to protect the full future value of our assets for ourselves, our children and our grandchildren? (We'll talk more at length about *market return* investing in Chapters 5 and 6.)

We will now look closer at the concept of stock picking, and why, like market timing, security selection techniques are largely an exercise in futility.

PICKS IN THE POPULAR MEDIA

To illustrate the ineffectiveness of the stock picking game, we turn to the print media. In the August 14, 2000 issue of *Fortune* magazine, billed as the "Special Investors Issue – The 2000 Guide to Retire Rich," there was an article entitled "Ten Stocks to Last a Decade," by David Rynecki.[2] This quote was contained therein:

> "…Fortune first identified four sweeping trends that we think have the potential to transform the economy … So for help in finding the stocks best positioned to capitalize on these four trends, we sought out some of the top stock pickers in the country … We also did our own due diligence by poring through financial statements, talking to companies, and giving their products a test run. The result: ten stocks that we think will be winners over the coming decade. We've included some household names but also a few surprises. They all share exceptional management and an ability to execute no matter what happens in the macro-economy – characteristics we think will be even more important if the economy slows and investors put a premium on those companies that post consistent numbers."

This information gives a credible and serious impression. Phrases such as "sweeping trends," "top stock pickers" and "due diligence" sound very important and official. Figure 2.2 shows the 10 stocks chosen and their price changes from August 1, 2000 through December 31, 2003.[3]

Figure 2.2

Stock	% Change
Genetech	23.02%
S&P 500	-22.29%
Viacom Class B	-33.07%
Univision	-36.11%
Morgan Stanley DW	-36.58%
Nokia	-61.36%
Oracle	-64.81%
Charles Schwab	-67.22%
Broadcom	-84.83%
Nortel	-94.30%
Enron	-99.96%

Data Source: MSN Money

Now notice that all but one of the selections lagged behind the S&P 500 Index by a significant margin. The group had an abysmal combined *annualized* return of **– 20.9 percent** for the period. Enron in particular is not likely to offer much help to the group in the near future.

OH, THOSE ATTENTION GRABBING HEADLINES

A second example takes us to the grocery store check-out line, where few investors can ignore the magazine headlines that call to them like siren songs. One such headline that we've tracked since June 1999 was from *Money* magazine. The cover title was "The Best 100 Mutual Funds – The Only List You Need."[4] The June 1999 date allows us to observe the performance of these "select" funds at the tail end of the bull market run through the bear market of March 2000 to November 2002 and into the up market of 2003. As of December 31, 2003 here is the "tale of the tape" of the last five years:[5]

2	funds no longer exist or have been merged into other funds
21	funds changed their name by 2004
93	funds are *actively* managed
31	funds have 12b-1 (marketing) fees
35	advertisements in this issue placed by the fund families chosen
71	funds disappeared from the *Money* "Top 100" list by 2003
5.35 percent	annualized average return for five years ending December 31, 2003
59 percent	funds beat their five-year annualized benchmark
57 percent	average fund turnover ratio
1.08 percent	average fund expense ratio

As we can see, the mutual funds fared much better than the previous individual stock example. This is witness to the greater amount of diversification that comes with mutual funds.

However, a closer look at the "Best 100" begs some interesting questions. Where are the two "best" funds that disappeared? Why did 21 funds change their names? Also, about half of the funds beat their benchmark, which means almost half *did not*. It was basically a coin flip. The overwhelming majority (93 percent) were *actively* managed (which is also indicated by the higher expense ratios and turnover ratios). We will see a little later how a *Market Return Portfolio*™ can mitigate most, if not all, of these difficulties.

We must concede that these two media examples were chosen to make a point concerning stock picking in general. Furthermore, we realize that there are possibly other publications that recommended winners during these very same time periods. With that said, however, consider this: With all the various opportunities to get "advice" from the media, which source(s) should investors use? Even if we assume that most of the pickers did provide good selections in the short run (and that is an enormous assumption!), we have seen no evidence that they can do it for extended periods of time – the way investors need them to. Additionally, if capital market returns are available without taking the risk of selecting the right picker, as we will soon re-assert, then why take the unnecessary risk?

A further concern is that information of this nature offered in a publication does not address personal issues relating to tax brackets, liquidity needs, family situations and the like. This speaks to the problem with interpreting mass media information as individualized advice. Unfortunately, most investors do not stop to consider this aspect.

PICKING MUTUAL FUNDS

Figure 2.3 shows the frustrating task investors often face when choosing mutual funds based on ranking services.[6]

Figure 2.3

	Fund A	Fund B	Fund C	Fund D
Morningstar[a]	★★★★★	★★	★★★	★★★★
Forbes	C	A	A+	D
U.S. News & World Report[†]	34	50	10	93
Wall Street Journal	E	C	A	B
Business Week	A	No Rating	B+	C

[a] Five stars is highest rating, one star is lowest rating

[†] 100 is highest rating, 1 is lowest

Observe that these are all respected rating services. The companies employ very bright, honest people trying to apply their skills to rating funds for investors. But note the disparity among the rankings of these actual funds.

Morningstar and *Business Week* loved Fund A. The other three (*U.S. News* in particular) did not like it at all. Fund B was a favorite of *Forbes* but evidently did not impress anyone else. Fund C was also liked by the analysts at *Forbes* and the *Wall Street Journal* but no one else (*U.S. News* apparently hated it!). Fund D was ranked high by *Morningstar* and *U.S. News* but the others rated it as average at best.

According to this information, which funds should investors add to their portfolios?

Obviously, this diversity of opinions presents a problem for investors who are relying on the "experts" to help them make selections. We are confident that hard-working intelligent analysts are making these judgments. The trouble is they are all using *different criteria* to make their assessments. So now, rather than just taking their word for it, investors are forced to judge who is using the *best* criteria in their rating methodologies. Who among us is qualified to undertake this task?

We would submit that we could take almost any fund in the mutual fund universe and find a similar variety of opinions. This situation as it exists is indeed frustrating for those seeking help. Unfortunately, oftentimes investors simply take the word of only one organization's ratings and move on. This can leave their portfolios quite vulnerable. We would guess that the overwhelming majority of mutual fund investors (and their advisors) make their decisions based on the confusing information just as we have detailed. But there is a better way. Stay tuned.

THE CEO FACTOR

Let's say for a moment that your professional money manager buys and sells individual securities in your account on a regular basis. An in-depth analysis on a particular stock has been done. Your money manager understands the company's business model; knows its products and has talked to its suppliers and the management team. In fact, your money manager has even conducted technical research on the price movement of the stock. It looks like a great stock and you are ready to buy, but you've forgotten one unknowable that could ruin your investment; the CEO factor.

The CEO factor has become a critical variable in the stock picking game. Some people may contend that this factor has always been present. But certainly with the advent of problems reported in the media, such as those with Enron and WorldCom, it is now undoubtedly a factor to be considered. Whether the problem is phantom revenue, mislabeled expenses, hidden loans or fictitious companies, these games can make all of the research useless and cause the stock price to plummet overnight. No amount of information can help an outside speculator if the leaders on the inside aren't playing the game fairly. So how do investors deal with this factor?

There are two primary risks in owning a stock. One is the systematic risk inherent in the stock market as a whole – called market risk. We cannot avoid this risk if we choose to own equities – and equities are the only way for the individual investor to create long-term wealth. Hence, investors must accept market risk.

The second investment risk is classified as non-systematic or individual stock risk, which is where the CEO factor looms so large. The solution to this risk is diversification – holding a multitude of stocks within each asset class in your portfolio. This does not change the risk in any specific stock you own, however, it does minimize the influence on your whole portfolio if one stock plummets. But how many stocks do you need to be sufficiently diversified?

How about all of them?

FUNDAMENTAL STOCK ANALYSIS

Fundamental analysis is a favorite of stock pickers. In fact, the overwhelming majority of security analysts consider themselves fundamental analysts. You may recall that *technical analysis* involves using historical data to devise market timing strategies. *Fundamental analysis* takes a different approach.

Fundamental analysts care little about the past price pattern of a stock or market and would rather focus on determining the proper inherent or fundamental value of a company. This involves trying to figure out what a stock is really worth. The idea here is to make some definitive distinction between a stock's current price and its *true* value. Analysts will pore over past financial numbers trying to estimate future earnings and dividends; they will take a close look at all the various financial ratios and conduct personal interviews with management during site visits. These activities will supposedly give analysts the tools they need to do the job well and determine if a buy, sell or hold recommendation is warranted.

However, in a study conducted for the National Bureau of Economic Research (NBER), the authors found that market analysts correctly predicted price targets slightly more than 50 percent of the time (coin flip). Furthermore, when the analysts missed their targets, they did so by more than 15 percent on average and in some cases much more.[7]

The basic problem with the fundamental analysis approach is the fact that various factors are uncontrollable. This is a problem because:

- Financial data is historical in nature. Old numbers have questionable value for predicting the future. Continual revisions make the task even more daunting.
- Market risk comes into play. That which affects the market as a whole may override any predicted pricing based on the value assessment of one company.
- Analysts are human. They may just miss on their assessment in spite of accurate data.
- The CEO factor is real. Even with perfect analysis, an unscrupulous executive may sink the whole company. Enron and WorldCom could be considered examples of such.
- Consistency is important. If the methodology *is* successful once, can analysts be successful again and again – to the extent that they must be in order to populate a properly diversified portfolio? The data overwhelmingly suggests they cannot.

Stock	% Change
Zebra Technologies	48.48%
Xerox	39.68%
Market Return Equity Portfolio	33.41%
CSX	22.57%
Pogo Producing	22.16%
Waste Management	18.02%
S&P 500	15.09%
Pioneer Natural Res.	15.00%
Air Prod. & Chem.	8.41%
Pfizer	6.47%
DuPont	-7.08%
Johnson & Johnson	-13.54%

Data Source: MSN Money; Dimensional Fund Advisors

However, if rather than buying this group of stocks, investors had taken a structured approach that offers the broadest and deepest diversification possible (i.e. a market return approach) they would have earned 33.41 percent during this same time period.[12] That is a big difference. On $1 million dollars that is a difference of $174,100 in one year. Furthermore, the standard deviation (which measures volatility or risk) of this broadly diversified Market Return Portfolio™ strategy would have been much lower because of the super-diversification. The chance of Fortune's individual stocks excelling consistently over time vs. the MRP™ approach is very small. Why? Simple. With MRP™ you can invest in practically the entire market. With only 10 picks you speculate and cast your lot on their futures alone.

THE HIGH COST OF PICKING

The Wall Street Journal reported in November 2003 that the average expense ratio for actively managed stock mutual funds had risen to 1.59 percent.[13] This was up from 1.54 percent the prior year. Costs considered in the expense ratio can include office space, staff, custody fees, legal fees, advertising, shareholder servicing and distribution fees. Although costs vary, some researchers have estimated that marketing expenditures constitute over half of all mutual fund expenses. This compares with using a market return strategy where the average fund expense ratio would be less than 0.50 percent.[14]

If that were the only comparison, it would be bad enough. However, there are other costs associated with stock picking and active management that are not always easy to understand. For example, trading costs are typically not included in the expense ratio although they may be buried somewhere within the prospectus. Incredibly, some funds can even have brokerage commissions as large as their expense ratios. Oftentimes, payments termed soft dollar arrangements provide payments to mutual fund sellers resulting in increased commissions. Trading costs and soft dollar arrangements can erode the performance investors ultimately receive.

Another menacing return stealing culprit is the bid-ask spread. Stocks have an ask price, which is the purchase price, and a bid, or sales, price. The difference between these two is known as the spread. Foreign and small cap funds have a typical spread of 1 percent to 4 percent, but the spread may reach into the 10 percent range because these are more difficult to trade. Large company stock spreads can be as low as 0.3 percent, but may exceed 1 percent as well. Add all this to the mix, and expenses – stated or not – can soar.

DO YOU ENJOY THOSE SUPER BOWL COMMERCIALS?

One of the most enjoyable aspects of the Super Bowl for many people is the fierce competition among commercials. Who can forget the herding cats, Michael Jordan playing H-O-R-S-E off of tall buildings with Larry Bird or the 1984 commercial by Apple Computer? Each year the ads seem to get funnier, more clever and certainly more expensive. The ticket price for the game has climbed from $10 for Super Bowl I in 1968 to $600 for Super Bowl XXXVIII in 2004. Likewise, a thirty-second commercial in 2004 had an estimated cost of an incredible $2.2 million.

Well, this is fine unless you see your mutual fund company run an ad. If you do, hopefully it will be entertaining, because you just unwittingly helped pay for the most expensive 30 seconds in television. Those advertising costs are passed through to shareholders – that means you. Worst of all, this expense does little or nothing to benefit current shareholders but rather benefits the fund company's effort to recruit new customers. So enjoy the game. But afterward you might make a note to check on your mutual fund expense ratios.

MISALIGNED INTERESTS

Another consideration involves the objectives of the fund managers. When you have a clear understanding of their goals, then you can easily understand why the total cost of active management is so onerous. When new money for a fund is raised via good *short-term* performance, it leads to a bonus or a raise in salary for managers.

Funds that perform poorly do not raise as much money and are eventually phased out along with their performance records (more on this later). The managers of these poor funds may try to make up ground by changing the composition of their holdings, which can get very expensive for the shareholders as we just discussed. Ultimately, these high costs are a result of what we call *misaligned interests*. That is, the investors/shareholders and the investment product providers and fund managers do not share the same objectives. We will deal with these misaligned interests in more detail in Chapter 4.

SPLITTING THE DECK

There is an old stock broker's trick that works something like this:

The broker places "cold" calls to 100 people. He asks 50 of them to invest a nominal amount in a certain stock – say ABC Company. This "recommendation," he states, is based on "carefully analyzed data of the firm and the industry sector using the very best fundamental analysis techniques." He reiterates several times the unique qualifications his analysts have in this particular niche. The story is compelling. (Never mind the unusual rapidity with which he tells this story.) The 50 unwary investors follow his recommendation.

The same broker then calls another 50 investors and recommends a different company – say XYZ Company. He tells a similar story and the investors follow the advice – again he asks for only a nominal investment at this time.

Perhaps a month later, when a winner between the two stocks has emerged, the broker then calls 25 of the 50 investors who hold the better performing of the two previous stocks and makes another recommendation with the same type of story. To the other 25 he makes a different recommendation and follows the same procedure. The 50 investors who hold the loser of the two original recommended stocks are ignored forever.

This "splitting the deck" technique is followed until at last the broker has three investors who have received five winning "hot stock tips" in a row from this "brilliant" broker and his "analysts." The broker then asks the investors to make a substantial portfolio commitment given his obvious expertise in the stock picking arena. And so the illusion of the expert stock picker proliferates.

The above example has many victims – not the least of which are the three remaining "winning" investors who have put their faith, and now their money, with this broker. The 97 who were ultimately ignored are actually quite fortunate in the end as they were no longer on the "hit list."

This is an extreme hypothetical example of how this technique works. But this manipulating technique is used in more subtle forms throughout the investment industry. Splitting the deck successfully raises money for the broker because of the undying hope most investors have to find that special person who can pick winning stocks.

WHY STOCK PICKING DOESN'T WORK

1. Choice conflict. This is not hard to understand. How many times have we been in a restaurant and had 50 choices on the menu? Don't we tend to select the same meal over and over again at a particular eating establishment because the choice is comfortable? When given too many choices we tend to fall back into a comfort zone and go with something familiar or make no choice at all. Stock pickers do the same. They tend to gravitate to familiar names that have been around. They follow the crowd, and this rarely offers a superior return. Fund managers who do this tend to fall into the same trap because their funds look much like each other and cause *overlap*.

2. Overconfidence. *Hindsight bias* is lethal in the speculation world. As humans, we all tend to look at the past and say to ourselves – "I knew that was a good stock." We then fool ourselves into thinking we should be able to pick the next one correctly. Or perhaps we get a few picks right and believe that speculating is an easy trade to master. One of the most dangerous things that can ever happen to a stock picker is early success. This overconfidence is a very common financial behavior characteristic. And it can be devastating.

3. Who is right? Analysts watch each other. Stock trading is much like any other business where individuals are trying to stand out with some hot recommendation. They know that investors have extremely short memories and therefore will tend to forget the bad selections as long as hope is restored with an occasional winner. Just take a look at financial magazine sales. They would not print the "best picks" lists if consumers did not buy them. Unfortunately, only a few of these opinions can be right at any one time. As a stock picker, or manager, it is an almost impossible task to be right very often. Therefore, to whom do we listen?

4. Corporate malfeasance. Dubious accounting methods and illegal conduct by corporate executives adversely affects companies and

markets. Enron is the poster child for this type of problem. How did so many analysts (basically all of them) miss this one? While this type of conduct has most likely always been present to some degree, in recent years we have seen an increase in the frequency of citations and indictments. This may be in part due to the gluttonous excess brought on by the good times of the bull market followed by the bear market of 2000 to 2002. In other words, the tide went back out and many were caught swimming naked. Therefore, even if investors could gain an advantage with the very best analysis and due diligence, the investment can end up a disaster because of one human indiscretion.

5. Efficient Markets. We cannot get away from this reality. The fact remains that for a picker to find a security that has somehow flown below the radar of the thousands of market analysts and landed in our own little portfolio – or that of our active fund manager's – it can most likely be attributed to random good fortune rather than skill. And to think that an entire fleet could be found on a consistent basis is nonsensical to any right-minded person.

SUMMARY

The obvious question we must ask at this point is: "Why do stock pickers do it?" Investment professionals who propose stock picking as a winning strategy are generally very bright people. Some may have not been exposed to the data that discredits their methods and are honestly trying to do what is in the best interest of investors. It is also likely, however, that many of them are well aware of the data but are so entangled in the system that provides their living that they do not feel they can leave it. Propping up active management is a personal financial decision for many advisors – not one made in the best interests of their clients. In other words, they must give the illusion that they are doing something (timing and/or picking) to earn their fees or commissions rather than seeking the best strategy for their clients. Unfortunately, the financial services world is replete with conflicts of interest such as this. Chapter 4 deals with this area in more detail and will hopefully encourage advisors to take an honest look at the situation and consider the best approach for their client's success.

In conclusion, investing in a manner that will accomplish broad capital market returns is highly preferable in the long run to a speculative, active management strategy that attempts to select or "pick" winners.

Chapter 3
Chasing Returns

T*iming* and *picking* are the unhealthy habits that lead to an insidious investing disease known as *chasing returns*. At the root of this malady is the hope and belief that higher returns can be caught by using these (failed) methodologies. But chasing higher returns is an almost sure road to investment failure. Good performance tends to disappear about the time the investor arrives. Chasing returns will result in consistently buying high and selling low – the exact opposite of any investor's objective.

Consider the following story to illustrate the concept:

On January 1, 1927, Fae Future had $1 to invest any way she chose. Having been born with the ability to tell the future, she naturally chose the correct place to put her money. Fae was able to do this very same thing for the next 76 years. That is, at the beginning of each year, she would invest her accumulated portfolio totally in the asset class that would be the winner with the highest return the *next* year. It is no surprise that rarely did one asset class have a long string of superiority. In fact, only once did one asset class have the highest return for four years in a row. None had it three years in a row. On nine occasions the best asset class had a two-year run. At any rate, Fae was about as successful as one can possibly be as an investor.

Consequently, Fae Future's $1 grew to approximately **$468,000,000** by January 1, 2003.

On December 31, 1927, Paul Past also had $1 available to invest any way he chose. Unfortunately, Paul was not blessed with the same psychic abilities as Fae. He had to look back at the previous year's results and choose the asset class he felt was the best. Not surprisingly, Paul always chose the asset class that had just finished the year with the highest return (Fae's choice twelve months earlier). How much did this hindsight approach net Paul at the end of the 76 years?

A whopping **$1,211**.

Remember, Paul did not invest in the *worst* asset class each year – he chose the asset class that had just finished *first* the year before. He also had the benefit of the 10 occasions when Fae's asset class selection had multiple year (2+) runs as mentioned. This means he was *also* in the best asset class of the year for 12 of the 76 years.[1]

This scenario is a microcosm of the return chasing game investors experience in every generation. Investors hope to be Fae Future. Yet knowing this is impossible, most investors make portfolio decisions just like Paul Past.

LOSING THEIR FAIR SHARE

Studies have shown that investors will receive, on average, less than half the market return on their portfolios. The diagram on the following page shows the profound negative effect that higher fees and the methodologies of active management (timing and picking) have on performance. During the period from 1982 to 2002, the S&P 500 Index had an annual rate of return of 13.1 percent compared to 10 percent in the average equity mutual fund. This resulted in the growth of $1 to $11.50 and $6.70, respectively. The average fund investor, according to estimates, earned only about 2.0 percent per year. This results in a minimal 50 cent profit over the 20 years.

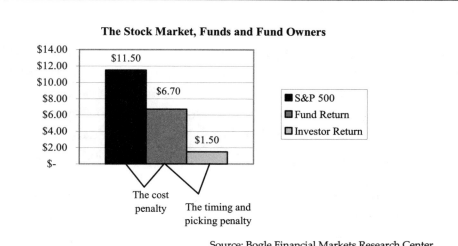

The Stock Market, Funds and Fund Owners

- S&P 500
- Fund Return
- Investor Return

The cost penalty

The timing and picking penalty

Source: Bogle Financial Markets Research Center

These bad results are compounded further when inflation and income taxes are taken into account. How can all this be? The answer is simple: chasing returns.

The endemic nature of this chasing ailment in America makes it a critical topic to thresh out. As previously discussed, media "hot lists" are so prevalent because editors and programmers are aware of this addiction investors have for predicting outcomes. It should be expected that speculation in the securities market is rife with the "get rich quick" mentality. After all, in similar fields of speculation, such as horse racing and other sports betting, the mindset is the same. People want to win big by predicting outcomes.

The trouble is, in the investing world, the media and Wall Street are so highly skilled at feeding this desire through *active marketing* that success in this realm appears to be reality. Trust us when we say, "This is *not* reality." If it were, this book would not have been written. Rather we would long ago have been reclining on the beach with our Fae Future newsletter subscription in tow.

FUND INCUBATION

Former Chairman of the Securities and Exchange Commission, Arthur Levitt refers to the aggressive mutual fund advertising of past returns as a part of the "culture of performance."[2] This suggests a systemic problem that is not easily overcome. Performance is nearly every investor's first criteria. Investment product vendors, knowing this, spare no expense in their advertising campaigns. They know as well as anyone that past performance is no indicator of future results (which is why such a disclaimer is required on any piece of investment sales literature.) However, they are in a very competitive business. Their job security and any promotions hinge on the constant attracting of new dollars to their funds. When the returns are not there to advertise, the easiest course of action is often to close the fund and move on. This leads to a discussion of another of Wall Street's games known as fund incubation.

The incubator fund strategy works something like this: A fund company opens up several new funds, each with an "appealing" strategy. For example, they may rely heavily on market timing, data mining or the next fair-haired manager with the golden touch. After this process runs its course, odds are one or two funds have hit a random hot streak and shown impressive one-year returns. These survivors can now be marketed and promoted for their high performance. The money then starts flowing in. After large amounts have been gathered, the high-risk issues are dropped and replaced with lower risk stock positions. This technique can eventually result in creating a closet index fund that maintains reasonable performance. Sound a bit fishy? That's because it is.

These incubator funds also present investors with higher internal fund expenses due to high advertising costs and frequent trading in an effort to find the supposed winners and attract new money. This lab experiment ends up bulldozing investors.

The incubation of funds is another indication that managers do not practice what they preach; but simply are seeking to feed the return-chasing desires of the general public. They will tout long-term investing and then trade frequently searching for the right security mix for their funds. This focus on short-term results is rarely spelled out in the prospectus, per se. Numerous studies have shown that higher turnover in funds generally leads to below-average performance because of higher expenses.[3] Timing strategies also exacerbate this problem as they try to predict up and down market moves.

All this trading and timing results in higher costs passed on to the investor. And for what? So the fund company can generate more revenue at fund holder expense. This is a plain example of the misaligned interests that exist between Wall Street and individual investors.

THE DUMB STATE FAMILY OF FUNDS

In our never ending quest for definitive answers, our "crack" investment research team put together what turned out to be a phenomenal methodology for picking winning stocks for a hypothetical mutual fund family – the DUMB (Diversified United States Mutual Fund Balderdash) State Funds. Rather than waste time with fundamental analysis or stock charting, we simply created a single criterion that would allow us to beat every actively managed fund in the Morningstar universe of funds.

This "painstaking" research was hashed out in about 10 minutes. What we did was simply divide all of the stocks on the U.S. exchanges into state categories. The companies were placed into mutual funds based on their corporate headquarters' location. Naturally, we ended up with 50 funds in our incubator grouping. The winner turned out to be the Wyoming Fund, which we affectionately renamed the Cowboy State Fund. This fund had an incredible one-year performance of 168.2 percent for the calendar year 2003. This was good enough to have beaten every one of the 2,121 actively managed U.S. mutual funds[4] with their "sophisticated" timing and picking strategies. These results would now allow us to blow our horn and advertise our tremendous results in every major media forum in the country and gather piles of investor dollars.

DUMB State Family of Funds

Rank	Fund Name	1 Yr Total Return	Rank	Fund Name	1 Yr Total Return
1	Wyoming Fund	168.22%	26	Michigan Fund	64.10%
2	Oklahoma Fund	156.79%	27	Nevada Fund	61.84%
3	Arizona Fund	147.15%	28	Louisiana Fund	60.93%
4	Colorado Fund	145.18%	29	Connecticut Fund	60.81%
5	Utah Fund	140.44%	30	North Dakota Fund	60.65%
6	Washington Fund	118.33%	31	New Hampshire Fund	59.53%
7	California Fund	109.83%	32	Pennsylvania Fund	59.04%
8	Massachusetts Fund	106.61%	33	Maine Fund	58.81%
9	Georgia Fund	103.73%	34	Arkansas Fund	56.90%
10	Florida Fund	103.41%	35	Iowa Fund	55.50%
11	Minnesota Fund	99.78%	36	Alabama Fund	55.36%
12	Oregon Fund	91.87%	37	Tennessee Fund	50.69%
13	New York Fund	90.48%	38	Wisconsin Fund	48.89%
14	Alaska Fund	87.02%	39	Delaware Fund	47.92%
15	North Carolina Fund	86.37%	40	Nebraska Fund	47.83%
16	Idaho Fund	86.21%	41	Indiana Fund	45.93%
17	New Jersey Fund	84.17%	42	Kansas Fund	45.66%
18	Texas Fund	83.27%	43	West Virginia Fund	45.30%
19	Mississippi Fund	78.40%	44	South Carolina Fund	43.92%
20	Hawaii Fund	77.73%	45	Ohio Fund	43.78%
21	Illinois Fund	71.63%	46	New Mexico Fund	42.91%
22	Maryland Fund	69.73%	47	Missouri Fund	41.15%
23	Virginia Fund	66.37%	48	Montana Fund	30.07%
24	Rhode Island Fund	65.99%	49	South Dakota Fund	29.54%
25	Kentucky Fund	65.93%	50	Vermont Fund	22.21%

Data Source: Morningstar Principia Pro

What does this exercise tell us? First of all, if you see a real active manager with superior results in the short run, it is quite likely to be plain dumb luck. Secondly, this exercise shows how one ridiculously simple and random criterion can outperform the best funded investment management teams available. Thirdly, the fact that we used only a one-year timeframe gives it little credibility. The Cowboy State Fund is likely to be at the bottom of the heap in a few years if it follows the pattern of other mutual funds that use stock picking and timing techniques.

As crazy and unthoughtful as this approach sounds, we concluded we had a proprietary idea – "dumb" as it was. Believe it or not, we found out after the fact that this approach is actually being used already. There are mutual funds that actually do invest only in companies of one particular state as part of their unique strategy.

P.S. This is a "tongue in cheek" example. The Wyoming Fund does not actually exist. Sorry. We know you return chasers are disappointed.

HIDING THE BAD EGGS

Another area that is little publicized in the active management world is that of survivorship bias. Survivorship bias occurs when mutual funds fail to perform and are swept under the rug like so many dust bunnies. This can be a byproduct of fund incubation or just plain bad performance. At press time, there were 16,527 mutual funds in the Morningstar database.[5] According to the Wall Street Journal in March of 2004, mutual funds continued to close and/or merge at an astonishing rate in the previous three years. They reported that 4,117 funds were either merged into other funds or closed in the combined years of 2001- 2003.[6] This eliminated over 4,000 track records that were quite likely below average. When these track records are purged, the average returns on all remaining funds go up – thus skewing the average and creating the survivorship bias.

Incredibly, during this same three-year period, an additional 6,161 new funds were created. This mutual fund shell game makes it more difficult to get accurate performance information. So beware of vanishing funds and the survivorship bias their demise causes.

FIRST TO WORST

The chart below shows the results of the Top 10 U.S. equity funds in two four-year time periods, back to back.[7]

U.S. funds, total annual returns, %

TOP 10 IN: 1996-1999			Rank		SAME FUNDS IN: 1999-2002		
0	50	100			-100	-50	0
			1	841			
			2	832			
			3	845			
			4	791			
			5	801			
			6	798			
			7	790			
			8	843			
			9	851			
			10	793			

Source: Bogle Financial Markets Research Center

The results clearly show how fickle funds can be in different time periods. As the chart shows, the top 10 funds returned between 45 percent and 65 percent from 1996 through 1999. These are impressive results that would catch the attention of any investor. Imagine owning a portfolio of funds with this type of performance.

Unfortunately, the same 10 funds did a complete turnaround as they all plummeted to the bottom of the pack in the next four-year period. (In fact, fund #9 became the worst performer) This is your worst nightmare if you are a return chaser. Yet it would be hard to find an investor, or even a broker, who would fault a decision to buy these funds in January of 1999 based on those results.

Chasing these returns would have been devastating to any portfolio. Similarly, chasing any returns will likely be detrimental to a long-term investing objective.

CHASING MUTUAL FUNDS

Figures 3.1 and 3.2 illustrate what can occur when timing, picking and chasing returns collide.

Assume we have two mutual funds or money managers – "A" and "B." On day one, $100,000 is invested in each fund. At the end of year one, we see that fund "B" has performed much better, with $140,000 in

---

it (Figure 3.1). What is the emotional return chasing move an investor may make? Naturally it is to move all the money into fund "B." The next year we see a disappointing result with "B" as it loses 10 percent. The consummate chaser would move the $225,000 back to fund "A" (Figure 3.2). If this chasing pattern continued for the duration of the five years, the end result would be that the original $200,000 portfolio would become $190,575 (Figure 3.2). That is a geometric compound return of *minus* 0.96 percent. Staying the course in both funds would have provided a return of 8.31 percent and a total of $298,864 at the end of the period (Figure 3.1). That represents over 50 percent more dollars in the account!

Figure 3.1

Fund A	Year 1	Year 2	Year 3	Year 4	Year 5	Avg. Return	Geometric Return
Return	10%	10%	10%	10%	10%	10.00%	10.00%
Balance	$ 110,000	$ 121,000	$ 133,100	$ 146,410	$ 161,051		
Fund B	**Year 1**	**Year 2**	**Year 3**	**Year 4**	**Year 5**	**Avg. Return**	**Geometric Return**
Return	40%	-10%	25%	-30%	25%	10.00%	6.62%
Balance	$ 140,000	$ 126,000	$ 157,500	$ 110,250	$ 137,813		

Figure 3.2

Fund A	Year 1	Year 2	Year 3	Year 4	Year 5	Avg. Return	Geometric Return
Portfolio Value	$ 110,000	$ -	$ 247,500	$ -	$ 190,575	1.00%	-0.96%
Fund B	**Year 1**	**Year 2**	**Year 3**	**Year 4**	**Year 5**		
Portfolio Value	$ 140,000	$ 225,000	$ -	$ 173,250	$ -		

In addition to providing evidence that chasing does not work, this table also shows the importance of reducing volatility or portfolio fluctuations whenever possible. The arithmetic average for both funds in Figure 3.1 is 10 percent. However, the geometric return is 3.38 percent lower in the more volatile fund "B." Thus the actual dollars in fund "B" is $23,238 *less* than fund "A."

Note that these examples look at only five years. As we will discuss in detail in Chapter 5, all portfolios are long-term in nature with limited exceptions. Therefore imagine the difference in dollars over 20, 30 or 40 years with unwarranted volatility or return chasing dragging the balance down.

HIRING THE BEST?

There is a fallacy in thinking among return-chasing investors. They want to fire their money or fund managers after a bad year and hire one that has just had a good year. They tend to treat their portfolios as if they owned a pro sports franchise. Firing head coaches in an effort to find that "guru" who will take them to the championship is a matter of course in the sports world.[8]

It is the same in the investment world, only different. First of all, it's the same in that investors feel that by hiring the "best" money manager based on last "season," they can buy a winner. It is different in that head coaches actually do have some influence on their players – money managers have no influence on the securities markets.

By continuously firing and hiring money managers an investor is unwittingly firing a manager when the fund is down and hiring another when the fund is high. Does this sound right? Buying high and selling low? This is definitely not a game plan for investment success.

THE BIGGEST EXPENSE IS ACTIVE MANAGEMENT

Attempting to create returns that the public will chase is very costly. In Chapter 2 we briefly discussed just how high mutual fund expense ratios have climbed. Other not so well publicized costs are also involved. These "soft" costs are worth mentioning in this context.

Morningstar data indicates that the average turnover ratio for actively managed domestic stock funds exceeded 109 percent for 2003.[9] This means that if there were 100 stock positions at the beginning of the year, they would have all changed by the end of the year. This level of trading is one good indicator that a manager is picking and timing.

Suppose that picking and timing could "beat the market," and thus provide an investor justification for chasing returns. Besides the hard costs that drag down returns, the chances are very small that this winning advantage could be maintained for any length of time, if at all. Meanwhile, investors are stuck with the bill. That is, the bill generated by active management, which is the biggest expense of all to investors as they time, pick and chase returns on their way to inferior performance.

FUNDS PROSPER, INVESTORS CHASE

Figure 3.3 shows the inverse relationship between the performance of an actual U.S. large cap fund and the assets that are gathered from investors.[10]

Figure 3.3

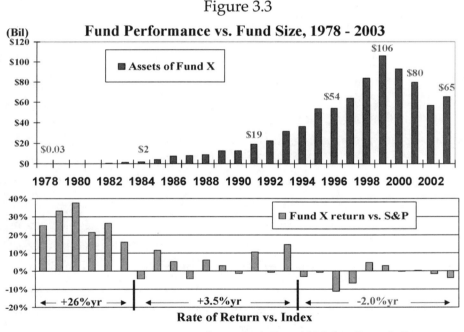

Source: Bogle Financial Markets Research Center

This is a clear indication of how the return-chasing mentality of most investors can be preyed upon by the mutual fund industry. By the time investors figure out the returns are no longer present, years have passed and many dollars and opportunities have been lost.

TACTICAL ALLOCATION

Evidence that timing, picking and chasing do not work has been more broadly accepted by many fund managers concerning individual stock positions. However, a form of chasing is still embraced by many – including investment advisors. Known as *tactical asset allocation*, this is the idea that specific asset class allocations can be timed.

Tactical asset allocation involves surveying the landscape on a *macro* level in order to determine the best place to invest at the moment. Shifting all or a part of a portfolio from small to large U.S. companies or from international value to growth categories are examples. While this concept can certainly be couched in a way that appears to reflect much consideration and planning, it still smacks of timing. If *timing* is present, *picking* and *chasing* are almost always involved as well.

A strategic allocation based on needs unique to each investor remains the right prescription. This includes the consideration of risk preference, cash flow needs, health issues and family situations (among others). Once analyzed, these should be used to create an *Investment Policy Statement (IPS)* that outlines the proper allocation strategy. If a change in a personal situation occurs, the allocation may *then* warrant a review and possible adjustment. Otherwise, the IPS will prevent, or at least discourage, ad hoc revisions in a long-term investment game plan. This is a very effective way to avoid the temptations that active management places in front of investors who might be tempted to employ tactical allocation techniques.

BORROWING TROUBLE

Active portfolio management with its timing, picking and return-chasing activity will ultimately provide plenty of trouble for its disciples. In some cases, the extreme desire to win in the securities lottery will create far more trouble than one can even imagine.

Take homemaking icon Martha Stewart. She dominated headlines as she struggled for acquittal in her stock trading case in 2002-2004. Stewart was not charged with insider trading. Technically, she was not an "insider" because she was not employed by the company whose stock was in question. However, she was charged with wrongdoing concerning her sale of the stock.

Regardless of the outcome of the case, it is astounding to contemplate the negative effect this incident had on Stewart's fortune. In comparison to the wealth she had before the event (easily in the nine or 10 digit range), this five figure transaction seems insignificant. Yet, this overwhelming desire to "get an edge" in the securities markets through active trading is common among investors at all levels. The situation is even more intriguing when it is considered that Ms. Stewart once had a career as a stockbroker.

This situation can be avoided when investors employ a structured *market return* approach to portfolio management. To put it another way, you should be an *investor* instead of a *speculator*.

The practices of active management can promote emotional behavior that is a danger to all investors. It is truly amazing to see the power of "picking and timing," when even people trained in the securities business cannot escape its allure.

WHY CHASING RETURNS DOESN'T WORK

1. Randomness. Active management seeks to achieve what is by nature random. Another way to put it: Active management depends on plain dumb luck. And any gambler knows that good luck is "hit and miss." Achieving good fortune *consistently* is not possible in a system that intrinsically cannot provide it.

2. Timing. Whether it is a rabbit, a baseball or a common cold, in order to *catch* something, timing is everything. As we have seen, timing the market is futile because of human shortcomings.

3. The System is self-serving. The *active marketing* employed by the investment industry is counterproductive because it entices

investors into buying its best performing products of *yesterday*. These misaligned interests bring its purveyors profits, while investors usually get only heartache and failure.

SUMMARY

The evidence presented concerning active management is sufficient to create serious misgivings about a dubious system. Investors who continue to apply active management methods adhere to Albert Einstein's famous definition of *insanity:* "doing the same thing over and over again and expecting different results."[11] The results *cannot* be different for the active manager/speculator as long as the ineffective methods of timing, picking and return chasing are used.

The first three chapters of this book were designed to give investors a synopsis of why active management, at its foundation, is a failure. This popular system, which promotes emotional behavior, is a danger to all investors. We believe far more money has been lost because of this culprit than all the accounting and trading scandals combined throughout history. At the heart of the matter is the continued systematic training of representatives who propagate the failed philosophy of active management, dooming their clients to investment returns well below what the market offers freely. In spite of the Wall Street juggernaut, we remain steadfast in our goal to educate as many willing listeners as possible to the proper way to invest.

CHAPTER 3

4 Chapter
The Financial Services Industry

The headlines in recent years make it clear that the financial services industry is experiencing many difficult challenges. Scandals involving corporate governance, mutual fund trading, and investment research analysts have made investors more cynical. And well they should. These shortcomings exemplify the system's flawed nature. While a protracted discussion of these issues may be interesting to some, we prefer to deal with these issues as they concern individual investors. Therefore we will examine the industry as it currently exists at the user level. In other words, at the system's point of entry – the investment advisor.

Investors are familiar with the traditional brokerage system that has been in place for many years. This system has been the bastion of the active management techniques as discussed in the previous chapters. The Wall Street goliaths of the industry have dominated the marketplace with overwhelming media power and lobbying abilities for decades. The situation has become especially confusing as these "Old Line" wire houses have joined the fee advice bandwagon over the last 5 to 10 years. Many brokers now offer fee-based investment advice along with commission-based products.

This change in the stockbroker world, along with other changes, makes it difficult to determine the difference between one financial service professional and another. There has been a commingling of core competencies that confuses the general public. The fact that nearly all the representatives working in the industry now call themselves "financial advisors" adds to the mystification.

In times past, bankers were bankers, insurance agents sold policies, brokers sold stocks and CPAs gave tax advice. This was the environment for decades because of longstanding federal securities laws enacted largely in response to the stock market crash of 1929.[1] This legislation separated the industry players. But, to a large degree, these legal barriers have been removed in recent years. Consequently, everyone is in one another's "back yard." From the point of view of the investor, this is not a good thing.

FIDUCIARY ADVISORS VS. BROKER FACILITATORS

The crucial issue that must be addressed when seeking professional financial advice is the role that the advisors are willing to take in the relationship. Are they willing to act in the manner of a *fiduciary* or not?

Most brokers and financial representatives are regulated by the National Association of Securities Dealers (NASD) and must simply adhere to a rule widely referred to as the *suitability rule*. This rule generally requires that brokers make a *reasonable* effort to gain appropriate financial information from a client before making specific investment recommendations.

A *fiduciary*, by contrast, is generally defined as an individual or organization that has a special relationship with the duty toward another individual or organization to act "in the highest good faith" and "with integrity."[2] Arthur Levitt, former chairman of the Securities and Exchange Commission, defines a fiduciary as an, "individual entrusted with investment decisions on behalf of another who is obligated to make decisions in the client's best interest."[3] For the purposes of our discussion, we will consider fiduciaries to be those willing to *act in the best interests of their clients and to disclose any real or implied conflicts of interest.*

A fiduciary standard is generally considered more stringent and broader than the NASD suitable sale standard. With this in mind, what investor would not rather have the more strict parameters in the relationship provided by a fiduciary? Clearly, removing conflicts of interests – what we call *misaligned interests* – will enhance the advisor's ability to offer objective advice.

There remains a line – although blurry – between most financial service representatives and fiduciary advisors. We take the position that once an advisor has held themselves out as an expert and a particular financial strategy has been recommended, the relationship should be considered fiduciary in nature. But whether or not brokers or advisors actually *are* fiduciaries in a legal sense is largely an issue for the courts to decide.

Due to the reality that the words *broker*, *representative* and *advisor* are often considered interchangeable, too many investors fail to realize that most in the financial services industry, in spite of their 'advisor' title, are basically sales people. As representatives of investment product manufacturers, they may be more loyal to their employers or suppliers than to their clients. This arrangement also tends to make them more likely to become order takers or *facilitators* for financial product vendors rather than true financial advisors. This divided loyalty begs the question: Who do you want investing your money? *You* should be your advisor's only focus.

Advisors who are willing to act in a fiduciary manner give their first loyalty to the client. The client pays the advisor *directly*. There are no *soft dollar* arrangements (as discussed briefly in Chapter 3.) There are no bonuses or trips to the Caribbean for selling certain products. There is no "Big Brother" looking over the representative's shoulder and influencing objectivity.

This *direct pay* fee arrangement greatly increases the chances that the advisor and client will have their interests in alignment. Furthermore, the direct pay system better allows the client to quantify the true value of the relationship. Think about it. How do you know the true value of something when you cannot accurately ascertain its cost? Direct pay alleviates concerns over the hidden charges that so frustrate investors.

The remainder of this chapter is designed to equip you with the knowledge and questions you need to ask when interviewing and engaging the proper type of investment advisor.

ACTIVE MARKETING

Forget active management and its failed methodologies. What Wall Street firms actually do excel at is the ability to make investors believe that the firms have what is best for clients. We've coined a phrase for this – we call it active marketing.

Part of this marketing shrewdness involves appearing all-knowing regardless of the market's direction. As brilliant marketers, those involved in active marketing are always in a position to develop new products that will be the answer. Their advice seems to shift as quickly as the wind as they are always at the ready with newfangled solutions. Unfortunately, most of these solutions are more beneficial to the product manufacturers and representatives than the clients they are intended to serve. Once again, we see the misaligned interests between the client and the investment firm.

Active marketing is especially common when it comes to proprietary products. Product manufacturers naturally will promote their own offerings to their representatives. Not surprisingly, these proprietary products end up as the recommendation all too often even though the representative may claim to be objective.

Proprietary investment products are especially prevalent in the areas of mutual funds, variable annuities and variable life insurance. Proprietary offerings tend to be more profitable to product manufacturers because they are able to cut out the middleman and distribute through their own corps of representatives. These products may have surrender charges that can last as long as seven years. This could mean that long after the product has stopped performing and the brokers have been paid their commission, the client is stuck. In addition, proprietary offerings tend to have higher expenses.

A successful portfolio can be built without using these products. By ignoring the Wall Street promotional juggernaut, investors do themselves an enormous long-term investing favor. Stay away from not only active management but also active marketing.

ALPHABET SOUP CREDENTIALS

What do these mean? CFS, CFP®, PFS, CLU, ChFC, CIC, AAMS, CIMA, CPA, CIS, CFA®, CRSP, MSFS, RIA, CMFC, CRPC. Believe it or not, these are all credentials available to financial services professionals. It is a small wonder why investors can get confused with this alphabet soup.

All of the credentials listed above are associated with worthy educational endeavors and are, to some extent, beneficial. However, in an effort to narrow down the field, we maintain that the *Certified Financial Planner™ (CFP®)* mark is one good qualifying denominator to consider when choosing an advisor. In the last decade this credential has become widely accepted as the financial planning industry's highest standard. It carries a three-year experience requirement and assurance of completion of a rigorous comprehensive exam covering all aspects of financial planning (including investing). It also requires continuing education on a regular basis (including ethics courses).

Another pertinent designating acronym is the RIA, or *Registered Investment Advisor.* This entity is registered with either the state securities department of jurisdiction or the Securities and Exchange Commission (SEC) depending on the amount of assets under its management. An advisor acting on behalf of an RIA is an Investment Advisory Representative (IAR). A Registered Investment Advisor is set up when fee advice is given by a firm. It does not necessarily designate an independent firm giving objective advice. Most brokerage houses now have RIA arms. The RIA should be considered a minimum requirement – not a certification of objectivity.

SEVEN ESSENTIAL QUESTIONS TO ASK WHEN INTERVIEWING AN ADVISOR

Choosing the right financial advisor is a critical, potentially life changing decision. Based on the previous description of how various entities deliver financial services, this list of questions is designed to provide a platform from which an investor can make an informed decision.

The following questions should be the minimum you ask a financial advisor:

1. Is your firm independent? The word *independent* can have different meanings. Therefore the answer to this question will almost always be "yes," initially, because any advisor knows the value the questioner perceives in an affirmative answer. The definition we are looking for in this context, however, is this: *having no association with any entities that adversely affect objectivity.* This list of entities could include banks, insurance companies, traditional wire (stockbroker) houses and broker-dealers (even "independent" ones).

We believe that a truly independent firm has no association with these organizations but rather is organized simply as a *Registered Investment Advisor* compensated with fees collected directly from the client. This arrangement gives the independent firm the ability to seek the best solutions for the client while minimizing the chance of a misaligned interest. This eliminates the pressure to push certain products (which is often associated with these parent company arrangements). The bottom line is that a representative (or, in alphabet soup terms, an IAR) of an independent Registered Investment Advisor can act in a fiduciary manner that eliminates conflicts of interest and applies the highest professional standard available to the client relationship.

2. How are you compensated and by how much? Financial advisors can be paid in several different ways: salary, commissions, flat project fees, hourly fees, percentage fees for assets managed, annual retainer or a combination of any of the above. None of these compensation methods are innately bad or good. However, in being consistent with our overriding consideration, when a client is working with an advisor, we feel that the fee arrangement has far less chance of producing a conflict of interest. In other words, an advisor who is compensated with fees – *directly* from the client – is not subject to being influenced by financial product vendors. Because the advisor is responsible only to the client for remuneration, he or she is likely to act in the best interest of the client.

Amounts for hourly fees, project fees and annual retainer arrangements can vary greatly. A comparison of two or three advisors would be a prudent course to take. Concerning the percentage charged for asset management, generally an annual amount of 1.0 percent should be the *high* end of any arrangement, with a lower percentage charged for larger portfolios.

3. What is your experience and what are your qualifications? Vernon Law once said, "Experience is a hard teacher because she gives the test first, the lesson afterward."[4] With that said, in the important area of money, it is not a good idea to allow someone to learn with *your* nest egg. The financial services industry is known for being an aggressive recruiter of inexperienced sales representatives. In fact, the average four-year retention of financial representatives is as low as 11 percent in some areas of the industry.[5] If a newer advisor is going to be considered, make sure the advisor has an established independent firm upon whose experience he or she can draw.

In addition to the minimum requirements discussed, seeking advisors who work specifically with people in your situation is very beneficial. There are many advisors who accept any client who successfully fogs a mirror, particularly when they are getting started in their careers. Ask for demographic data on the clientele of an advisory firm so you can see the firm's representatives are accustomed to working with individuals with your needs, objectives and problems. (If you need brain surgery, it is not wise to use a heart surgeon to perform the operation – brilliant as the heart surgeon may be.)

WHAT ABOUT ASKING FOR REFERRALS?

It is a natural tendency to want to visit with current clients of an advisory firm to get an idea of their level of satisfaction. Therefore, to ask for one or two referrals may be a good idea. Unfortunately, in the world we live in today, confidentiality laws may delay this process as the advisor will likely want to get permission from the current client before such an inquiry is made. Another problem with a referral request is the likelihood that you will be referred only to the advisor's very favorite clients (or maybe even a relative) who may give you a biased view.

There is an alternative that may give a more comprehensive view of the firm. Any reputable firm looking to improve service should be asking for evaluation and feedback from its clientele on a regular basis. When interviewing potential advisors, ask them for copies of their annual client survey. This survey should have been done so that the client identity is not revealed, thus allowing for candid responses. Typically, 30 percent to 50 percent of the clients will respond to a survey of this nature. If the firm indicates that it has 100 clients, then you should be able to view 30 to 50 surveys. There will likely be some negative comments on some of the surveys. After all, no one is perfect. In fact, clients may be more likely to return a survey when they have a complaint. If no negative comments exist on any of the forms, beware – you may be the victim of a "scrubbing" of the data. At any rate, the client survey approach can be an excellent way to get an indication of the quality of the firm you are considering.

---

4. What is your approach to providing financial advice? In the past, the majority of advisors have often offered investment recommendations without having sufficient facts concerning client goals, objectives and challenges. Any advisor worth their salt will recommend creating a written financial plan *before* offering any financial or investment advice. We *strongly* believe to do otherwise is simply malpractice. It is tantamount to receiving a prescription from your doctor without having been examined or diagnosed. This written financial plan can initially include a *retirement cashflow analysis,* an *investment policy statement* and a *risk management analysis*. Often, an *estate analysis* is also warranted.

Once this written plan is completed and analyzed, the implementation should proceed with recommendations concerning various investment options and risk management tools. Obviously, any investment advice that involves *active management* techniques, as discussed earlier, should be summarily dismissed along with the advisor. This is a good subject to broach *before* the written plan is started. It is foolish to have a plan created by an advisor who likely cannot implement it properly.

5. Does your firm use a team approach? The advice here is simple: Two heads are better than one. A common misperception is that larger financial firms are better by mere virtue of their size. However, in most cases, large national firms are government-like bureaucracies that actually only lease space to individual representatives in their offices. While a visit to the local branch may give the impression of a team approach, it is likely an organization with multiple solo brokers with perhaps a shared personal assistant. Ironically, smaller independent firms are usually better at building a team that can collectively devote their energies to a client's best interests.

Working as a true team means that all clients are clients of the firm – not clients of individual advisors within the firm. This also helps with continuity in the event something happens to specific advisors where they are no longer part of the firm. Additionally, in smaller independent firms, the owners/principals are usually involved in the client relationship directly.

6. Will you provide in writing a description of the specific services you are recommending? Whether they are providing financial planning or asset management services, registered advisors should be prepared to provide a written sample agreement for your review in an initial meeting. This should include the delivery of a Form ADV, Part II (a document required by the Securities and Exchange Commission that provides pertinent information concerning the background and detailed operation of the firm and its principals and representatives). These documents will allow a prospective client the opportunity to compare what is said in an initial interview with what is in writing. If there is no willingness to provide such documentation, then simply walk away. This is not an advisor worth your consideration.

7. Are you willing to act in a fiduciary manner in this relationship? Because it is the central message of this chapter, we have saved this most important question for last. Most of the other questions in this list have implications concerning fiduciary responsibility. But there is no better way to get to the crux of the matter than by simply asking this question directly. Some representatives may not even completely understand the question or its implications. For reasons cited previously, this question is likely to disturb many of the brokers and representatives who *do* fully comprehend it. They are often in no position – either professionally or with their business entity structure – to take on the responsibility that an affirmative answer to this question demands.

No client should accept or expect anything less than the standard that is implied by an advisor being a fiduciary; "to act in the best interests of the client and disclose any real or implied conflicts of interest." Once again, if a potential advisor cannot answer this question with a swift and confident "Yes!" walk away.

BEWARE THE FREE LUNCH

We have all heard this warning a thousand times: "There is no such thing as a free lunch." Yet from time to time we all fall prey to the overused sales tactic of offering something for nothing. One approach popular in the financial services world is the "free" financial analysis. A broker will offer to create an initial analysis of your situation at "no charge." If anything appears amiss in the plan, the client can engage to have a complete plan done for a *nominal* fee or perhaps for no charge *if* the client agrees to implement the final plan with the broker. That implementation means buying financial products. The broker receives a commission, a fee, a trip to the Caribbean – you get the picture.

A conflict-free way of doing business is better for the investor. Advisors should take a look at a clients' financial data in order to assess the level of planning needed to assist them. Next, the advisor should be engaged *in writing* to complete the written financial plan on a flat fee or hourly basis. If implementation of the plan recommendations is desired after the plan is evaluated, the client then has an opportunity to make that decision separately. The *planning* and *implementation* phases should be separate services. This way the client can receive an unbiased plan with "no strings attached." That is, no obligation to invest or buy a product from the representative because of "all the trouble I went to."

SUMMARY

This chapter is intended to provide a clearer understanding of the financial services delivery system at the user level. We can assure you there are financial advisory firms in your community that adhere to the standards addressed in this chapter. As a client, you should not settle for anything less than a **perfect score** on this short list of questions. If an advisor gets only five or six right, move on. You deserve to have the finest help available. It is your financial well-being at stake, and choice of an advisor is a very serious decision that you *must* get right the first time.

In a nutshell, if you want to enhance the chances of having a successful financial advisory experience, look for a firm that:

- Is Independent
- Uses a fee structure where advisors are paid *directly* from clients
- Uses a *market return* approach
- Is team oriented
- And whose advisors are:
  - Experienced
  - Well educated (Preferably a CFP® professional)
  - Willing to operate in the manner of a fiduciary

Remember, this list is concrete and to be used in total. Unless the advisor and firm pass all the criteria, keep looking.

Always keep in mind that the advisor is not doing you a favor by managing your finances. The advisor is your paid employee. You are the boss. Never hire anyone but the best and most qualified candidate. Hire the best the *first* time around.

PART II:
WEALTH WITHOUT WORRY

"All truths are easy to understand once they are discovered; the point is to discover them."

– Galileo Galilei

5 Chapter
The Answer is Right in Front of You

Most of us remember watching *The Wizard of Oz* as children. We recall that moment when Dorothy and her ragtag group of traveling companions finally reach The Emerald City and stand trembling in the presence of the Wizard – that seemingly omnipotent power they have never seen or heard who holds their fate in his hands. And then, of course, we remember the disappointment. But what about that strange sense of relief we feel when the Wizard turns out to be nothing more than a nervous little man hiding behind a curtain? In the end, Dorothy learns that she had the tools to accomplish the very thing she desired all along – her ruby slippers. She then closes her eyes and chants, "There's no place like home, there's no place like home …"

It's time to pull back the curtain and reveal the truth. The wizardry of Wall Street is history. As an investor, you now have the ability to achieve just what you need and desire. Free markets are the means by which you can get "back home," financially speaking.

This leads us to the tenet that is the cornerstone of this entire book:

Market return is there for the taking.

When you fully appreciate this concept, it revolutionizes the way you think about investing as well as how you invest. Not only will it change your life as you no longer concern yourself with the best place to put your money, but this *market return* precept also allows you the opportunity to stop worrying about your financial *future* and live in your glorious *present*.

Eliminating this concern allows you the time and freedom to attend to the many things in life that are more important than money.

You may ask, "Why do I *want* market return?" Some investors are concerned about the risk involved in the stock market and shy away from stocks. Others are not satisfied with receiving *only* market return, thinking they can "beat the market." Therefore this question requires a two-part answer.

FEAR ITSELF

First of all, we'll speak to the group that is, to put it bluntly, afraid of stocks.

The long-term goal of investors should be to protect their *purchasing power* – or what we call the *cost of life*. In overcoming the insidious effects of inflation, stocks are by far the most effective and efficient tools to use. Figure 5.1 below shows the annual compound rate of return for some general asset classes over the last 78 years:

Figure 5.1

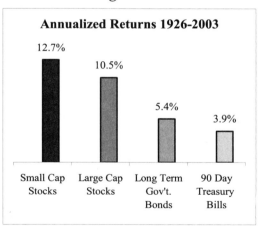

Data Source: 2003 Andex Chart

This graph shows the average annualized return of bonds to be approximately *half* that of stocks. The owners of stocks have clearly had the advantage.

When inflation is taken into consideration, the gap widens even further. This is known as the *real* rate of return. With inflation averaging **3 percent** during this timeframe, the return multiple for stocks changes from twice as much to *three* or *four* times as much as bonds. (Figure 5.2)

Figure 5.2

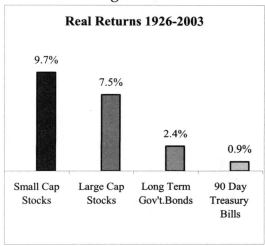

Data Source: 2003 Andex Chart

When we plug into this equation the higher marginal tax rates of bond interest (potentially 35 percent) versus the capital gains and dividend treatment (15 percent or even 10 percent at lower income levels) available in equities and translate the numbers into actual dollars, we have the makings of a *huge* gap (as seen in Figure 5.3). When the effects of inflation *and* taxes are brought to bear on a long term portfolio, the results show a definite advantage to holding stocks vs. bonds. (Income tax rates have fluctuated over the last 80 years. We used current rates to illustrate the point.)

Figure 5.3

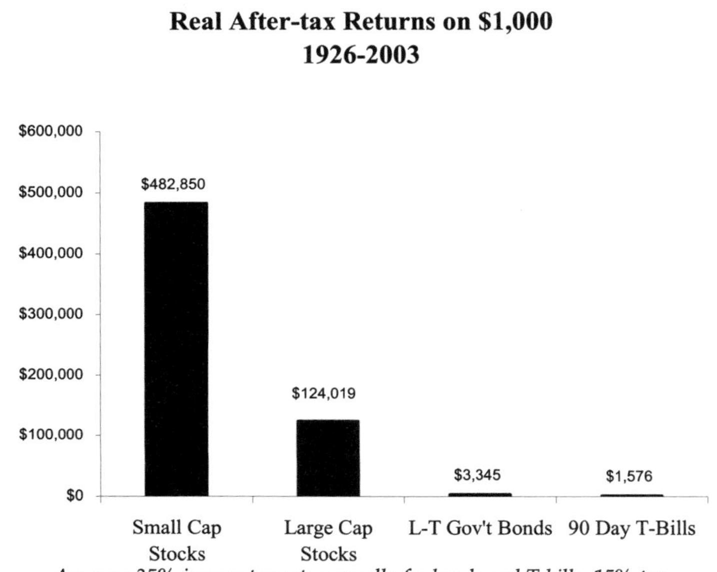

Real After-tax Returns on $1,000
1926-2003

Assumes 35% income tax rate annually for bonds and T-bills, 15% tax rate annually on capital gains for small and large cap stocks.

Data Source: 2003 Andex Chart

Even after seeing these numbers, many will say, "Stocks are still too risky for me." This sentiment is widely held – especially among investors nearing retirement age. But it's simply not valid.

This fear of stocks is born out of two misperceptions:

1. Investors do not understand the meaning of *long-term.*
2. Investors do not really know what true portfolio *risk* is.

WHAT IS INFLATION?

"Inflation is when you pay fifteen dollars for the ten-dollar haircut you used to get for five dollars when you had hair." Sam Ewing

Here's a quick question: Would you rather buy a one-year Treasury bond that paid 11.2 percent in 1980 or one that yielded 5.9 percent in 2000? The answer seems obvious – the higher yield is preferable. But believe it or not, the better investment was the 2000 Treasury bond, even though the yield was 47 percent less than 1980. The difference, of course, is the rate of inflation that investors were experiencing during each time period. Prices rose over 12 percent in 1980, while they climbed only 3.4 percent in 2000.[1]

WHAT IS *LONG-TERM?*

Almost all portfolios (with just a few exceptions) are long-term in nature. Exceptions would include portfolios designed to save for a down payment on a house, to pay off short-term business debt or those designed for putting money aside for a college education. In all of these cases, the money has an end point when it will all be used for a specific expenditure in a given timeframe. Even at that, the college education fund can and should be invested for growth – especially early in a child's life.

If a nest egg is needed for any type of income generation – it should be considered a long-term investment. With retirees living longer, this income may be needed for 30 or 40 years after retirement. The temptation for many people planning for retirement is to go to a large bond or fixed income position to "protect" the investment and get yield. Yet, as we have seen, the *total return* for stocks vs. bonds is not even close – especially when inflation and taxes are considered. Even money that is set aside for an inheritance should be positioned to grow and benefit the heirs for whom it is intended.

Whether we are in pre-retirement, retired or at a stage in our lives when we want to leave a legacy for our loved ones or a cause in which we deeply believe, all portfolios should be managed in such a way as to achieve real growth. That means planning for the *long- term* and using equities.

WHAT IS PORTFOLIO RISK?

With long-term thinking established, we turn our attention to the second part of the misperception concerning a fear of stocks – the real meaning of *portfolio risk*. The first definition of *risk* in most dictionaries is: *"the possibility of suffering harm or loss."* This is the definition that comes to mind for most investors who are afraid of losing their money – or their *principal*. In a proper investing context, we are not content to protect *only* our principal – but rather our purchasing power – which *encompasses* our principal and its future growth and income (i.e. *total return*).

As we dig deeper into the list of dictionary meanings for *risk* we discover this additional definition: *"the variability of returns of an investment."* The word *variability* is a beautiful word to investors who are seeking *market return*. Variability means *"the quality, state or degree of being variable or changeable."*

Most people generally dislike change and often assign a negative connotation to it. However, when things are *changeable,* the potential to become better also exists. Change does not inherently connote a negative. When we invest we *want* changes. Why? Because the vast majority of the time, change in a securities market is a *positive* experience – not negative! (See again Figure 2.1) Therefore, if we can embrace the power of change and realize through a study of ample data that free markets *must* grow over time – then we can have confidence that taking on all the risk the market has to offer means we have a greater opportunity for positive *change*. Ironically and not intuitively, herein lays the basis for *genuine* portfolio protection.

WARS AND RUMORS

Whenever we are at war, the prevailing question investors ask is, "What effect will a war have on my portfolio?" While the question may be largely unanswerable, it is somewhat helpful to look at the effects that armed conflicts have had through the years. The chart below shows the annualized returns of two major U.S. market indices[2] the year a conflict actually occurred as well as in the following three-year period:

Conflict:	Time Period	S&P 500	Small U.S. Co.
World War II	1941	-11.58	-10.03
	1942-1944	21.96	45.61
Korea	1950	31.74	38.25
	1951-1953	13.27	6.41
Cuban Missile Crisis	1962	-8.73	-17.43
	1963-1965	17.17	22.89
Vietnam	1964	16.51	17.14
	1965-1967	7.84	30.42
Desert Storm	1991	30.55	48.83
	1992-1994	6.26	11.56
Iraqi Freedom	2003	28.69	58.46

Data Source: Dimensional Fund Advisors

First of all, we can make some general observations. The effects in the year the conflicts began have varied. The stock markets were largely negative in the year World War II began and during the Cuban Missile Crisis, but were up considerably the years each of the other four conflicts began. However, it is difficult to draw much of a conclusion from this information given the fact that both WW II and the Cuban incident took place late in their respective calendar years. Secondly, and perhaps most significantly, the average three-year period returns following the year the conflicts started, were all positive; with most up significantly.

This data suggests a couple of things. Number one, it could be argued that the effects of war on the economy were either already factored into the markets or became factored in early in the conflict. Number two, while the news from each conflict was at times very bad, it was still only one factor in the world's most powerful economy, which is affected by numerous other economic factors each day.

The conflict with Iraq may most closely resemble Desert Storm for obvious reasons. It may also contain some similarities with the Cuban Missile Crisis, which was technically not an armed conflict. However, it was an alarm clock that awoke the American consciousness. While the Cold War was at full throttle in 1962, it was also an ocean away. The Cuban crisis brought the threat of ending the American way of life within 90 miles of our shore – a wakeup call, to say the least. Even though the crisis was averted, the threat remained firmly imbedded in the psyche of our society from that point on. Yet capital markets rose over the next three-year period (and beyond).

There is no reason to believe that a free economy and free markets will do anything other than survive and ultimately thrive after any future conflicts – unless we are unwilling to protect freedom (and thus free markets) when threatened. The irony is that the only way economic survival and prosperity is maintained in both times of war and times of peace is to protect the freedom we hold so dear. This has always enabled us to recover.

THE RESILIENCY OF THE STOCK MARKETS

How can we gain confidence that change will usually be a positive experience? The key here is to understand the positive effects that time has on money invested in free markets. For example, if you were to look closely at the S&P 500 index over the last 78 years you could easily see how time in the market mitigates negative downturns and has proven positive the overwhelming majority of the time. Meaning, over the long haul, it continues an upward trend.

Figure 5.4

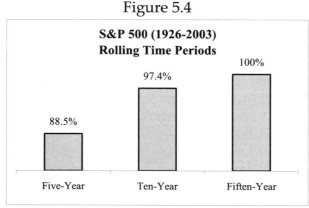

S&P 500 (1926-2003)
Rolling Time Periods

Data Source: Dimensional Fund Advisors

CHAPTER 5

As seen in Figure 5.4, when we look at any five-year *rolling* timeframe, positive returns occur nearly 90 percent of the time. When 10-year or 15-year rolling timeframes are observed, positive returns occur 97 percent to 100 percent of the time! Furthermore, since the Great Depression (1929 to 1932), the S&P 500 index has *never* had a four-year period of time when it lost ground each year. The most recent three-year losing streak was from 2000 through 2002. However, just like clockwork, 2003 came roaring back growing a healthy 28.7 percent.

With this incredible track record in mind, consider all of the events that have occurred since the 1920s: two World Wars, the Korean War, Sputnik, the Cuban Missile Crisis, the assassination of President Kennedy, the Vietnam War, President Nixon's resignation, hyper-inflation, Iran hostages, oil embargos, Black Monday, the Persian Gulf War, President Clinton's impeachment, the terrorist attack of 9-11 and the Iraq war. Furthermore, three of these events in particular had a sudden and shocking impact on the psyche of the American people and on the securities markets. The surprise attack on Pearl Harbor was instigated by a rogue nation in search of global dominance. The Kennedy assassination was carried out by a supposed lone gunman of counter political persuasion. The 9-11 attacks in New York and Washington were perpetrated by terrorist groups not affiliated with any single sovereign government.

While all of these events were different, all threatened the very fabric of our society; and in the case of Pearl Harbor, even the *existence* of our society. These events had a negative impact on the stock markets. The chart below shows the number of days it took the Dow Jones Industrial Average to recover to pre-tragedy levels.

Tragedy	Date	DJIA Closing	Days to Recover
Pearl Harbor	December 7, 1941	112.52	334
Kennedy Assassinated	November 22, 1963	711.49	4
9-11	September 11, 2001	8920.70	59

We can see that the recovery from these horrific events was relatively short as the billions of daily economic factors took control and overcame the negative effects. Capital markets are resilient even in the very worst of circumstances.

2003: ANOTHER CASE IN POINT

When we consider the results of the equities markets in 2003, how could anyone have ever predicted what would transpire? Consider the following: the SARS epidemic from Asia, the start of the Iraq war, the plunging U.S. dollar, the mutual funds scandal, continued malfeasance in major corporations, and reports of an overall weak economy with slow job growth. Yet in the midst of all of this, a stock investor would have had to be completely unlucky to earn less than 25 percent. The large cap U.S. stocks had their best year in the last five, large international stocks had their best in the last 17 and micro cap stocks had their best year in 36 years.[3]

The Dow Jones Industrial Average hit its low on March 11th at 7,524 and then proceeded to climb almost 3,000 points by the end of the year. Investors were naturally nervous early in the year due to all the bad news. There are many who stayed on the sidelines watching as the bad news continued and the stock market climbed. The lesson: get in and stay in. Bad news and events will have an effect on the markets, but they will recover.

No other nation or economic system has ever existed like the one we are blessed to be a part of now. In light of this phenomenon we call capitalism; *optimism* is the only logical reality. Fear of loss should be replaced by hope of change. Hence, investors can see investment fluctuations in a whole new light. You should no longer mistake *variability* for *loss*, and you should desire to have *market return* through positive market *change*. Given this paradigm, we can now argue that *stocks are actually safer than bonds* when our objective is to protect our long-term financial cost of life.

Does this mean we should never own bonds in our portfolios? No. We'll talk more about their proper role in a later chapter.

THREE'S A CHARM?

When investors are in the middle of a bad market cycle they tend to assume that the next year will be the same as the last. This is a dangerous assumption to make. History punishes *return speculators* time and again for being poor market extrapolators. Consider this: The most difficult stock market periods in the last century have been the Great Depression (1929-1932), Pre-WWII (1939-1941), Post Vietnam (1973-1974) and the post tech bubble bear market period (2000-2002). However, we see that both bad *and* good markets come in spurts of three years or less, with only a few exceptions. One exception is the 1929-1932 period of four bad years. Another is the more recent 1995-1999 *bull* market, which lasted five years. Other than these, it is difficult to find an asset class with longer periods of distinct ups or downs.

The other interesting piece of data in relation to the short-term behavior of markets is the fact that when the trends shift in the other direction, they do so with whiplash speed. For example, during the 1939-1941 decline, the S&P 500 *lost* an average of 7.4 percent per year. In 1942-1944, it subsequently *gained* an annual average of 22 percent. In 1973-1974, it *lost* an average 20.8 percent each year but *gained* an average 30.4 percent the next two years (1975-1976). For this same time period, the turnaround was even more dramatic for small cap stocks: a 35.2 percent *loss* and 62.0 percent *gain* respectively. For international companies, the index dropped an average 18.2 percent each year, only to rebound with an average *gain* of 19.2 percent during 1975 to 1976.[4] The real winners in the long-term investment arena will be those who stay the course by diversifying their equities among multiple asset classes and accepting the returns that will inevitably come. To borrow from Abraham Lincoln: "Let no feeling of discouragement prey upon you, and in the end you are sure to succeed."

THE "MARKET BEATERS"

As we mentioned earlier concerning the question, "Why do I *want* market return?" there are those who ask this question with the idea in mind that they can "beat the market." Therefore, they are not interested in settling for anything less. But over any significant period of time it is not only unlikely, it is *highly* improbable that anyone can consistently beat *market return*.

In the first half of the book we spent considerable time discussing *active management* techniques and their failings. We explained how *timing* and *picking* lead to a belief that an investor can chase returns successfully. The reality is that the overwhelming majority of active managers actually end up providing *less* return than the market would freely give. In order to drive this point home once and for all, we will engage in a little exercise in probability.

WHAT ARE THE ODDS?

If *market return* is truly *there for the taking*, then the ratio of our chance of getting *market return* would have to be 1:1. Stated differently, we would have a 100 percent (one out of one) chance of getting *market return*. Exactly how *market return* is achieved will be discussed in the next chapter. (But for now, we will work under the 1:1 assumption.)

Before we can answer this completely, we would submit that proper portfolio diversification demands that we invest in at least *four* different stock asset classes. For example: large U.S. growth companies, large U.S. value, small U.S. value and large international. (Note that asset classes are not the same as *sectors* such as technology, utilities or biomedical.) Most likely, we would use somewhere between six to 15 asset classes *including* bonds. However, for our discussion, four will easily make the point.

By researching all of the various mutual fund managers in the universe, we find, as shown in Figure 5.5, how many active managers in each category beat their market benchmark (or index) in 2003.[5]

Figure 5.5

Asset Class:	Funds	Beat Index	%
Large U.S. Growth	395	133	34
Large U.S. Value	279	88	32
Small U.S. Value	89	22	25
Large International	257	83	32

Data Source: Morningstar Principia Pro

As you can see from the chart, 34 percent of the active large U.S. growth company managers beat their benchmarks in the one-year period. The ratio or chance of this being accomplished therefore is about **one out of three.** The other three asset classes achieved percentages of 32 percent, 25 percent and 32 percent, respectively, in the one-year period. The next question we would ask is: "What are the chances that we could pick active managers who beat their benchmark indices in each of the four asset class categories for the one-year period?" The calculation is as follows:

$$.34 \times .32 \times .25 \times .32 = 0.8704\%$$
or 1:114

What does this mean? It means that you have a 1 in 114 chance of finding money managers that can beat the market in each of the four asset classes. This compares with a 1 in 1 chance of getting *market return* in all four. So which is more attractive? Keep in mind we are looking at the probability of achieving this in just *one* year.

What about the probability of stringing the last 5 or 10 or 30 years together to build a portfolio that consistently "beats the market" each year? Here are the numbers in the same asset class order as in Figure 5.5.

5 Years: .052 × .015 × .035 × .06 = 0.000164% or 1 in 610,501
10 and 30 years = LOTTERY-LIKE ODDS

The numbers become unrealistic.

As we saw in Chapter 3, chasing returns is a natural tendency among investors who seek to "beat the market" using active trading techniques. The data here shows it is highly unlikely that such speculative habits would mesh with the buy and hold stance needed to patiently wait out a manager's poor years. Most investors would jump ship after one, two or certainly *three* bad years.

WHAT ABOUT *RISK ADJUSTED* RETURNS?

All too often investors focus on *return* and forget the importance *risk* plays in a portfolio. While it is true that taking more risk generally provides a higher return in the long term, we would suggest that you should only take the amount of risk necessary to achieve *market return*. (Racecar driver Johnny Rutherford once said, "The important thing is to win at the *slowest* speed possible.")[6] For example, if an active fund manager is beating his benchmark index, but taking 40 percent more risk than the market risk to do so, the *risk adjusted return* is likely not worth it.

Figure 5.6 shows the same results we discussed above when adjusted for *market risk*.[7] In other words, the same comparisons including only those managers who took the same or less risk than the S&P 500 Index and still beat their benchmark.

Figure 5.6

Asset Class:	Funds	B*<=1	%
Large U.S. Growth	395	28	7
Large U.S. Value	279	52	19
Small U.S. Value	89	14	16
Large International	257	59	23

Data Source: Morningstar Principia Pro

*B = *Beta*, a measurement of volatility or risk. Generally, the market risk is presumed to have a beta of 1.0. The higher the beta, the higher the risk.

As you can see from the chart, **7 percent** of the active large U.S. company managers beat their benchmark in the one-year period with equal or less risk than the S&P 500 index. The ratio or chance of this being accomplished therefore is approximately **1 out of 14.**

The other three asset classes achieved ratios of 19 percent, 16 percent and 23 percent respectively, in the one-year period. The chances that you could pick active managers that beat their benchmark indices maintaining market risk or less in *all four* asset classes for the one-year period is as follows:

.07 x .19 x .16 x .23 = 0.04894%

or 1 out of 2043

Clearly, the numbers are stacked against active management even further when this *risk adjusted* data is considered. This shows that the chances of achieving a diversified, lower risk, actively managed portfolio that beats the market even for *one* year is highly improbable.

The concepts we have just discussed are a testament to why we almost never see *actual* clients with *actual* portfolios that consistently "beat the market." We only see *individual* fund track records for a limited time *after the fact*. Since no investor owns only one fund (hopefully), it is the *portfolio* return that really matters.

WHAT WOULD *MARKET RETURN* ACTUALLY LOOK LIKE?

Investors should be beneficiaries of both the *protection* and *growth* that the markets freely give. To show these two very important aspects, we now introduce, in more detail, the concept of a *Market Return Portfolio (MRP)™*.

One market timeframe in particular gives us a wonderful laboratory in which to examine the benefits of getting *market return*. The years 2000 to 2003 were an excellent testing ground for such a protection and growth study. We saw the worst bear market since the Great Depression followed by a dramatic turn around into positive territory. Many market timers and stock pickers tout such periods of volatility as the perfect environment for them to apply their craft. Let's then compare the results in this interesting timeframe.

Figure 5.7 shows the results of stock indices during the bear market of March 2000 to November 2002. We'll call it the *Bear Chart*.

Figure 5.7

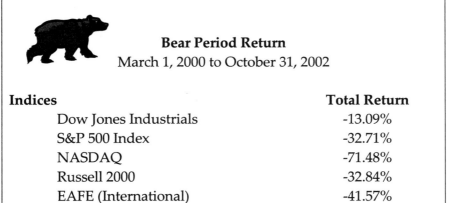

Bear Period Return
March 1, 2000 to October 31, 2002

Indices	Total Return
Dow Jones Industrials	-13.09%
S&P 500 Index	-32.71%
NASDAQ	-71.48%
Russell 2000	-32.84%
EAFE (International)	-41.57%
Market Return Portfolio™ Models	
Equity (100% Equity)	-8.95%
Aggressive (80% Equity)	-3.18%
Balanced (60% Equity)	2.67%

Data Source: Dimensional Fund Advisors; Morningstar Principia Pro

For the sake of comparison, we also tracked three *Market Return Portfolio ™* models.[8] As you can see, the MRP™ strategy was very effective at buffering the ill effects that this deep bear market created. We coined a term for this type of protection. We call it the *Giant Portfolio Stop-Loss effect*. We believe this is the result of the *super-diversification* found in the asset class funds used in MRPs (details are forthcoming in Chapter 6). Because the *Aggressive* and *Balanced* MRP™ models have some fixed income contained in them, the best "apples to apples" comparison is found when we look at the *Equity* MRP™ strategy, which is composed of 100 percent stock funds. As we can see, it *lost* only 8.95 percent during this 32-month period as the major stock indices plummeted in comparison. Imagine owning nothing but stocks during this deep bear market – and still only losing about 3.4 percent per year.

We next review the time period from November 2002 through December 2003. We call this our *Bull Chart* (Figure 5.8).

Figure 5.8

Bull Period Return
November 1, 2002 to December 31, 2003

Indices	Total Return
Dow Jones Industrials	28.01%
S&P 500 Index	28.25%
NASDAQ	50.67%
Russell 2000	51.49%
EAFE (International)	40.02%
Market Return Portfolio™ Models	
Equity (100% Equity)	50.25%
Aggressive (80% Equity)	39.74%
Balanced (60% Equity)	29.80%

Data Source: Dimensional Fund Advisors; Morningstar Principia Pro

This period shows a dramatic reversal from the previous 32 months. All the stock indices showed a marked improvement during these 14 months. Note that the NASDAQ index came back over 50 percent during this time period. However, the 71.5 percent it lost in the bear market meant that it had to gain over *200 percent* in order to reach its original level before the bear market began. This shows the *exponential* damage that can occur in difficult markets. This is why investors should be very aware of the *protection* element in their portfolio allocations, which is provided by *super-diversification*.

While we are generally looking to *match* market returns, the results of this chart surprised us at first when we saw the MRP™ strategies[9] outpace the major index averages. We do not, however, put much emphasis on this higher performance because this is a short sample timeframe to compare.

Upon further consideration though, we attributed this MRP™ out-performance to the *diversification effect* of the portfolios as the market quickly grew out of the bear market. We define the diversification effect as simply the concept that asset classes, once combined, have less risk and thus less volatility as the risk is spread. Figure 3.1, which we discussed earlier, shows this very clearly.

Figure 5.9 shows the two time periods we have analyzed in combination: March 2000 through December 2003.

Figure 5.9

The Composite Chart
March 1, 2000 to December 31, 2003

Indices	Total Return
Dow Jones Industrials	11.25%
S&P 500 Index	-13.70%
NASDAQ	-57.02%
Russell 2000	1.74%
EAFE (International)	-18.18%
Market Return Portfolio™ Models	
Equity (100% Equity)	36.81%
Aggressive (80% Equity)	35.30%
Balanced (60% Equity)	33.28%

Data Source: Dimensional Fund Advisors; Morningstar Principia Pro

Several interesting observations can be made. First apparent is the fact that three of the indices remained in negative territory even though the *bull* market had been in effect for 14 months. The deep losses experienced during the *bear* period have not yet been overcome. In contrast, the MRP™ models[10] have made their way *well* into positive territory. Once again, the protection element provided by the wide and deep diversification of the MRPs during the *bear* period, allowed them to avoid playing "catch up" to the same degree as the indices.

Additionally, the *extended market* also enhanced the performance in this time period. The *extended market* is the portion of the market not included in the indices. Many of these excluded companies are included in the institutional asset class funds used in the MRP™. (This concept will be discussed further in Chapter 6.) The ability to diminish the harsh effects of down markets can give the MRP™ strategy a distinct advantage.

Now if the indices faired in this manner, how did the *actual* mutual fund managers perform in this same composite timeframe (March 2000 through December 2003)?

Average *Period* Return for Actively Managed U.S. Stock Mutual funds: 1.26 percent[11]

Remember, this average is also subject to *survivorship bias,* which eliminates thousands of the underperforming funds that were merged or closed. The effect of *survivorship bias* would have driven this percentage even lower.

After seeing the data concerning these 46 months, it begs the question, "What about *longer* time periods?" Does the MRP™ strategy work well over the long haul? In this regard, Figure 5.10 gives the results of the 20-year period from 1984 through 2003.

Figure 5.10

20-Year Annualized Return	
January 1, 1984 to December 31, 2003	
Indices	**Total Return**
Dow Jones Industrials	14.28%
S&P 500 Index	12.99%
NASDAQ	10.63%
Russell 2000	10.19%
EAFE (International)	10.80%
Market Return Portfolio™ Models	
Equity (100% Equity)	14.94%
Aggressive (80% Equity)	13.60%
Balanced (60% Equity)	12.19%

Data Source: Dimensional Fund Advisors; Morningstar Principia Pro; Dow Jones

As you can see, the overall objective of receiving *market return* holds true for this longer time period as well. This chart shows a more normalized result for the MRP™ strategy[12] as it provides performance roughly equal (although somewhat higher on average in this sample) to the market on a *consistent* basis. *Consistency* – that "1:1" probability of getting a dependable representation of market performance – is the key element in the MRP™ methodology. Without this 1:1 component, investors are left twisting in the wind as they try to beat the lottery-like odds that active management offers. *Lack of consistency* is the Achilles heel of active management portfolio strategies.

A MULTI-TIMEFRAME COMPARISON

For further validation of a *market return* strategy, Figure 5.11 shows the 10-year *rolling* returns for the *Equity* MRP™ model, which is composed of stocks only. The diagonal shaded boxes represent the average annualized return for each rolling10-year period. Note that the annual average returns for all periods are in double digits with the exception of one (9.7 percent from 1993-2002). Imagine when it is all said and done making an average annual return of 11.2 percent during the 1994 to 2003 timeframe – which included that brutal bear market – and being invested 100 percent in stocks!

Also notable is how relatively few negative returns for *single* years there were for the entire 30-year period: a total of four in 1973-1974, 1990 and 2002. We believe this data, along with that previously noted, should give investors sufficient confidence that *market return* truly is *there for the taking* on a consistent basis with relatively low volatility. This is true, even with full exposure to the stock markets in a 100 percent stock portfolio.

Figure 5.11

Data Source: Dimensional Fund Advisors

SUMMARY

Investors must understand that protecting *only principal* is not enough. If you want to protect your financial *cost of life* for many years to come, use equities.

We have shown that the prospect of using properly diversified equities is not a scary one but rather an exciting one when the data is considered. This does not mean that investors can completely avoid periods of down markets. However, the fear should subside when it is understood that this *market return* and purchasing power protection is available on a *consistent* basis.

Additionally, the odds are incredibly low that investors can find even a few active managers who can "beat the market." The odds are lower still when you consider managers who take risk equal to, or below, the market risk. Given this evidence, why would *any* investor want to give up *market return* – especially when it is ***there for the taking***?

Finally, we saw how the *Giant Portfolio Stop-Loss effect* that a *market return* strategy provides can greatly buffer the negative effects of extreme down markets and thrive with the market (as a whole) in good times. The MRP™ methodology also works as expected by delivering *market return* during extended time periods covering several market cycles.

Remember that the probability of getting *market return* remains at 1:1. In the next chapter we explain how this can be achieved and how to successfully formulate a *Market Return Portfolio™*.

6 Chapter

Building a Market Return Portfolio™

As youngsters, most of us heard the Bible story of the wise man who built his house upon solid rock. The rain came down, the streams rose and the winds blew and beat against that house; but it did not fall because it had a firm foundation. Conversely, the foolish man built his house on sand. When the rain came down, the streams rose and the winds blew and beat against that house; it fell with a great crash.[1]

In the financial realm, the *Market Return Portfolio (MRP)™* strategy entails building our investment house upon solid ground that can withstand the economic storms that befall it. Why? Because it is built on the bed rock economic system of free capital markets. Building a portfolio using *active management* is tantamount to building a house upon the sand that will cause it to eventually collapse.

This final chapter is designed to give you more detail on just how an MRP™ strategy can be implemented. This will provide the confidence to move forward with the last investment strategy you will ever need.

THE ROLE OF DIVERSIFICATION

It is one thing to buy stocks when you realize that it is the only place to be in order to beat inflation and attain real growth. It is quite another to do it properly.

We have mentioned diversification throughout our discussion, but before we can explore more details of building a *Market Return Portfolio™,* we must define and discuss what *proper* diversification actually means. The key is *super-diversification,* so-called because it transcends or passes beyond the limits of commonly defined diversification.

Diversification is a concept to which nearly all investment advisors give lip service. Unfortunately, few actually ever apply diversification correctly. A classic example of improper diversification was seen in the mid to late 1990s when the buying of large U.S. stocks – particularly tech stocks – was all the rage. The media and most brokers and advisors were telling investors that the "New World Economy" had "changed" things. Consequently, they were inclined to be overly weighted in the hot sectors or flavor of the day. The "tech bubble" burst in 2000 and quickly brought them back to reality.

THE TULIP BUBBLE

Much has been made of the tech stock bubble bursting in 2000 and the adverse effects this had on improperly diversified portfolios – and rightly so. But as we study behavioral finance we see that this is a phenomenon not peculiar to our period or even our culture. (Once again proving the thesis that human nature has been, and always will be the same. This is good for MRP™ investors.)

Another bubble experience took place in the 1590s when events were put in motion in Holland that led to one of the most spectacular get-rich-quick binges in history. A Venetian botany professor brought a collection of unusual bulbs to Holland from Turkey. Over the next decade, the tulip became a popular but expensive item in Dutch gardens. When the flowers were stricken with a nonfatal virus known as mosaic, which caused colored stripes to develop on the tulip petals, speculation in tulip bulbs went wild. Popular taste dictated that the more bizarre the bulb, the greater the cost.

"Tulip mania" had set in. Bulb prices rose out of control. The more expensive the bulbs became, the more people viewed them as smart investments. Traditional industry in the country was dropped in favor of speculation in tulip bulbs. Everyone imagined that the demand for tulips would last forever and that people all over the world would pay any price for them.

People who claimed prices could not possibly go higher watched their friends make enormous profits. The temptation to join them was irresistible and few Dutchmen sat on the sidelines. In the last years of the tulip craze (which occurred from 1636 to 1637), people bartered their personal belongings, land, jewels and furniture to obtain the investment vehicle they thought would make them rich.

> As happens in all speculative crazes, prices eventually soared so high that some people decided they should sell. Soon others followed until a snowball effect took over. Panic reigned in no time. The government stated officially that there was no reason for tulip bulbs to fall in price – but no one listened. Dealers went bankrupt and most bulbs became practically worthless, selling for no more than the price of an onion.[2]
>
> The comparisons that can be made between this historical event and those experienced in the "tech bubble" are obvious and painful. How do investors avoid the doom of past mistakes? The answer is in the question itself – they become investors and not speculators.

Diversification is the most critical and misunderstood element of investing. Many believe they have proper diversification because they have multiple individual securities or mutual funds. Headlines similar to "How to Diversify with Only Nine Stocks" can add to the confusion.

Here are four problems associated with improper diversification:

1. Using individual securities. Very few investors have enough capital to diversify properly by purchasing hundreds or thousands of individual stocks. (And it does take that many, by the way.) They are lulled into believing that holding 30 or 40 stocks protects them from loss.

2. *Blue Angel* syndrome. This occurs when too many securities in the same asset class – either individual stocks or mutual funds – are held within the same portfolio. When the asset class is doing well, the positions all soar in precise formation like the Blue Angels F-18 flight team. However, when the market cycle turns, they may all crash together as well.

3. Overlap. Many investors understand that mutual funds help diversify from the *first* dollar. The mistake occurs when they fail to realize that many fund families have considerable overlap within the family of funds. This means that two differently named funds may hold many of the same securities, which undermines the diversification goal.

4. Dumping "bad" funds. This is simply the same as chasing returns. We tell investors that they actually *want* to see at least one of their assets classes doing poorly at all times. (Obviously not the same one all the time.) This indicates that they are properly diversified among asset classes because asset classes have dissimilar price movements. These divergent movements are the key to overall portfolio performance. Remember, you should not be concerned about *individual* fund performance because the asset class cycle will turn positive with time *if* given the chance.

As we saw in the bull and bear charts in Chapter 5, broad and deep asset class diversification mitigates the losses in bad markets. We called this the *Giant Portfolio Stop-Loss effect*. Now, technically there is no such thing as buying a stop-loss on an entire portfolio as one can on an individual stock position. But a *super-diversification* strategy basically provides that same type of safety net. *Super-diversification* also allows an opportunity to share in the market return when the bull market runs again.

The building blocks, or tools, we suggest using to accomplish *super-diversification* are known as *institutional asset class funds (IACFs)*. They allow investors to diversify properly among all the companies in a particular asset class, starting again with the *first* dollar.

INSTITUTIONAL ASSET CLASS FUND CHARACTERISTICS

The concept for institutional asset class funds (IACFs) was born out of Modern Portfolio Theory (MPT). The theoretical foundation for MPT was published by Harry Markowitz in 1952.[3] Along with two associates; Markowitz won the Nobel Prize in Economics in 1990 for his work on the subject. Other academicians gravitated to this logical process. Eventually, enterprising individuals implemented the MPT methods by creating the asset class funds now available for investors through independent registered investment advisors.

Institutional asset class mutual funds are designed to deliver the investment results of an entire asset class – such as large U.S. value stocks or small international. These asset class funds are best suited to create efficient portfolios that promote *super-diversification*.

There are four important characteristics of institutional asset class mutual funds:[4]

1. Lower Costs. The IACFs are true no-load funds. They have no front or back-end loads, redemption fees or 12b-1 marketing expenses. They are also 100 percent liquid at all times.[5]

All mutual funds have operating expenses. These expenses are expressed as a percentage of assets and include management fees, administrative charges and custodial fees. The average annual expense ratio for all retail equity mutual funds was around 1.59 percent in 2003.[6] In comparison, the same expense ratio for an institutional asset class portfolio was typically around 0.50 percent.[7] These lower costs naturally lead to higher net rates of return when compared with more expensive funds.

2. Reduced Turnover. The average actively managed mutual fund routinely has turnover rates in excess of 100 percent.[8] This is because they attempt to add performance by trading often within a fund. This high turnover means that if a fund holds 100 securities at the beginning of the year, at the end of the year all of them would have been sold and perhaps repurchased.

A high turnover ratio usually means that active management (timing and picking) is taking place. This high turnover is costly because, as discussed in Chapter 2, other hidden costs including commissions, trading spreads and market impact costs have a negative effect. These hidden costs can even amount to more than a fund's total operating expenses if the fund trades frequently or if it invests in a more inefficient market (such as small company or international stocks where trading costs can be even higher).

In addition, highly active investors can cause excess turnover by chasing after performance. They move from fund to fund looking for hot asset classes or managers. This can force fund managers to buy and sell even more often than they might like. These return-chasing investors do not pay their share of the transaction costs they create. They buy and sell at net asset value (NAV), freeloading on the backs of long-term investors who remain in the funds.

By contrast, institutional asset class mutual funds have low turnover rates. They use an objective *portfolio filter*[9] to determine holdings, which usually results in less than 33 percent turnover per year.[10] This keeps costs low, which in turn improves performance.

3. Tax Efficiency. Mutual funds are required to distribute 95 percent of their taxable income each year (including realized capital gains) to remain tax-exempt. Managers do not want to have their fund performance reduced by paying corporate income taxes. Therefore, they distribute all their income annually.

Taxable distributions can have a negative effect on the rates of return of equity mutual funds – particularly those that are involved in active management. The frequent trading that is utilized in an attempt to add value often results in short-term capital gains in a rising market. This means tax rates are in the 35 percent range potentially vs. the 15 percent (10 percent for lower incomes) long-term capital gains rate. Because asset class funds are holding their positions based on structured criteria, even the 33 percent turnover is typically more apt to result in long-term gains taxed at the lower 15 percent rate. This inherent characteristic provides much more tax efficiency.

4. Consistent Portfolio Allocation. Research has indicated that the largest determinant of portfolio performance is *asset allocation*.[11] In other words – how the portfolio is divided among different asset classes. Efficient asset allocation is accomplished when the mutual funds in your portfolio maintain their allocation integrity. Most active managers change their fund asset class percentages over time. They may change their composition by moving from growth to value or small to large or even stocks to bonds. In addition, they often increase or decrease their cash balances based on cashflow requirements and market situations. These ad hoc allocation adjustments, known as *fund drift*, create portfolio inefficiencies and can significantly change the composition of a portfolio over time.

By using active managers an investor will give up control of the asset allocation to the managers of the mutual funds. Since the managers do not know each investor's situation, they make allocation decisions based on *their* needs -- not the client's (misaligned interests). A distinct advantage of IACFs in this regard is that clients are able to maintain their asset class allocation exposures as documented in the investor's investment policy statement.

Now that we have discussed the building blocks themselves, we will combine the principles we have learned to build an efficient Market Return Portfolio™ model.

CREATING THE MARKET RETURN PORTFOLIO™ MODEL

Thus far we have considered at length the futility of active management. We have discussed the current investment advisory delivery system and what to ask when seeking an investment advisor. We then studied market return including the role of diversification and the building blocks of the Market Return Portfolio™ – institutional asset class funds. Now it is finally time to talk about building a portfolio that can allow *every* investor to triumph and create wealth without worry.

In order to best describe the Market Return Portfolio™ composition, we will compare it with a Diversified Index Portfolio (DIP) represented by familiar indices.[12] We will view results over a 25-year period from 1979 through 2003 as seen in Figure 6.1.

Figure 6.1
Diversified Index Portfolio (DIP)
1979-2003

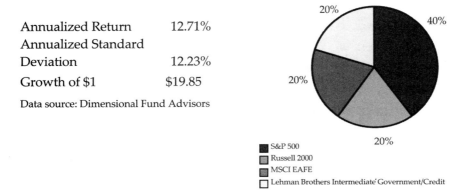

Annualized Return	12.71%
Annualized Standard Deviation	12.23%
Growth of $1	$19.85

Data source: Dimensional Fund Advisors

■ S&P 500
▨ Russell 2000
▨ MSCI EAFE
□ Lehman Brothers Intermediate Government/Credit

Knowing what you now know about stock returns vs. bonds, having a 100 percent equity portfolio should no longer be a scary proposition. However, most investors will ultimately require some fixed income in their retirement years. Therefore, we will use as an example a model that contains an 80:20 stock:bond ratio using four common indices of the S&P 500 and the Shearson-Lehman Government/Corporate Bond Index, Russell 2000 Index and MSCI EAFE (International). This type of allocation is fairly common among investors who are referred to as *indexers*. We like the indexing approach from the standpoint that it ignores ineffective active management techniques.

However, our objective is to create an 80:20 model that will bring about the *purest* representation of the market and thus truly be a portfolio that delivers the highest probability of receiving market return.[13] If the MRP™ approach either *increases* return or *lowers* risk, we consider it desirable. If it happens to do both, then we really have hit a "grand slam."

Figure 6.2
80:20 Market Return Portfolio™
1979-2003

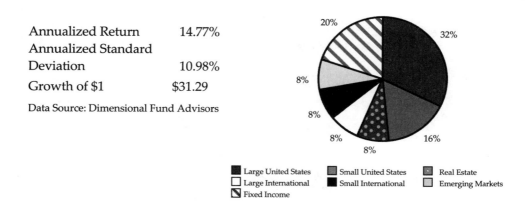

Annualized Return   14.77%
Annualized Standard
Deviation   10.98%
Growth of $1 $31.29

Data Source: Dimensional Fund Advisors

Legend:
- ■ Large United States
- □ Large International
- ◩ Fixed Income
- ■ Small United States
- ■ Small International
- ▦ Real Estate
- ▥ Emerging Markets

The first observation we can make as we compare Figures 6.1 and 6.2 involves the average annualized return. The Diversified Index Portfolio (DIP) returned an average of 12.71 percent per year for the period shown (Figure 6.1). Most investors who have memories of the bear market of 2000 to 2002 would likely be happy to sign a contract for that 25-year performance right now. However, the *80:20* MRP™ model shows a return of 14.77 percent per year – more than two percentage points higher than the DIP.

Before we look at just what this means to an investor in the way of actual dollars, we must first consider other expenses that come into play.

The average weighted expense ratio for index mutual funds to implement the DIP would likely be around 0.25 percent. We reduced the net annualized performance from 12.71 percent to 12.46 percent to account for this. Additionally, while the 14.77 percent return of the MRP™ already includes the mutual fund expense ratio, we must also subtract a fee for the independent registered investment advisor (RIA). By subtracting a fee of 0.50 percent, the MRP™ return is now reduced to 14.27 percent. With this in mind, the difference in return is now reduced to 1.81 percent in favor of the *80:20* MRP™ strategy.

Now 1.81 percent may not sound impressive to some investors. But what does that difference translate to in terms of dollars? Figure 6.3 shows the effects of this difference on a $100,000 portfolio over 25 years.

Figure 6.3

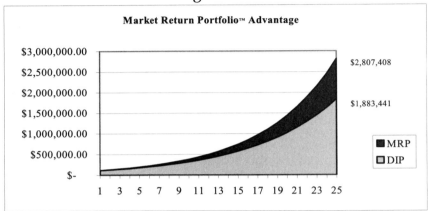

The $100,000 in the *80:20* MRP™ would have grown to just over $2.8 million vs. about $1.9 million for the DIP. That is a difference of almost $1 million, or 49 percent *more dollars.* This clearly shows how valuable small percentages can be over time. (And remember, most portfolios should be considered *long*-term. There are few exceptions.) For fun, we also looked at the same for a $1,000,000 portfolio. What was the *difference* in 25 years? A whopping $9.2 million *more* in the *80:20* MRP™ model.

In Chapter 2 we spoke of shifting your paradigm concerning the way you should think about your portfolio (10+ million vs. 1 million). With market return being *there for the taking,* the numbers above should make you keenly aware of what you are giving up if you choose *not* to participate in that which is rightfully yours in a free capital market.

Additionally, the MRP™ strategy would have delivered this substantially higher return at the same time it exposed the investor to 10.2 percent *less* risk. (This is measured by the *standard deviation* or volatility of each portfolio:10.98 for the *80:20* MRP™ vs. 12.23 for the DIP.)

More return, less risk. Exactly what every investor desires and deserves.

THE EXTENDED MARKET'S REAL VALUE

It should be restated at this point that the primary MRP™ objective is to simply mirror, as closely as possible, the return and risk of the market. It's worth repeating that whenever there is additional return, it occurs largely because of the wide and deep *super-diversification*.

On this point, consider the following: The MRP™ institutional asset class funds hold a combined 15,169 individual stock holdings. The DIP represents 3,432 securities.[14] This is a difference of 11,737 or over 340 percent more exposure to the market. This exposure to an additional 11,737 companies is also what we referred to as the *extended market* (as discussed in Chapter 5). This is where you can gather a bit more return – return that can add up to a significant amount of dollars over the long term. It also means that even when a major collapse occurs, such as with Enron or WorldCom, it is but the very tiniest "blip on the radar screen" of such a vast number of holdings in the entire Market Return Portfolio™. *Safety in numbers.*

THE ALLOCATION PERCENTAGES

We will now take a closer look at the specific asset classes that make up the *80:20* Market Return Portfolio™ model.

FIXED INCOME ASSET CLASSES

On the fixed income (or bond) side of the equation, the asset class funds used to construct the MRP™ model are primarily short-term (less than five years) in nature because longer term bonds generally entail more risk with a diminishing return. This is because bonds have an *inverse* relationship to interest rates. As interest rates climb, bond values decline and vice versa. Figure 6.4 shows this risk:return relationship. The longer the duration of a bond, the greater the risk, and thus the greater the potential decline. By holding shorter term bonds, you can reduce the erosion of principal in rising interest rate periods and maintain a stable portion of the portfolio for income generation. We included both U.S. and global bond funds in the *80:20* MRP™ to provide further diversification.

Figure 6.4
Short-Term vs. Long-Term Bonds
Quarterly: 1964 to 2003

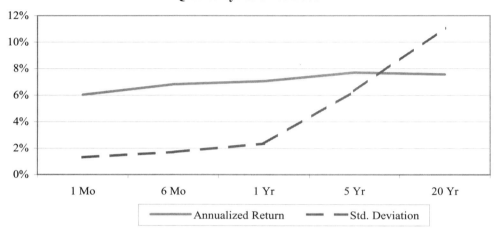

Data Source: Dimensional Fund Advisors

U.S. EQUITY ASSET CLASSES

The equity (or stock) portion of the allocation has three general areas. As we saw in Figure 6.2, 32 percent of the entire portfolio is made up of large U.S. company funds. These are equally divided between *blend* and *value* funds. Small U.S. funds make up 16 percent of the allocation, equally divided again between blend and value.

Finally, a real estate asset class fund (or REIT) contains 8 percent of the allocation. (Depending on the status of real estate ownership outside their portfolio, not all MRP™ investors will have a REIT fund in their allocation. For example, if investors own rental properties in addition to their homesteads, the REIT allocation may be deleted. This determination should be made on a case by case basis.)

INTERNATIONAL ASSET CLASSES

International market exposure makes up the remaining 24 percent of the portfolio, with the large value, small company and emerging markets each accounting for 8 percent of the allocation.

It is very important to include foreign exposure in a portfolio. Investors often ignore international markets because they regard them as too risky. This is a mistake. Investors also tend to believe that if they own domestic companies that sell products or services overseas that they are investing internationally. Research indicates that stock prices of companies tend to follow the trends of their domiciled country even if a majority of their business comes from foreign markets.[15]

International markets tend to move in different directions than domestic markets. When we say "different," this may mean that they are both going up or down, but at a different pace. In the case of foreign markets led by Japan in the mid to late 1980s, we saw a good example of times when international markets outperformed U.S. markets by a wide margin.[16] Diversification into foreign markets during this and other timeframes has preserved capital for many an investor. Typically, a super-diversified Market Return Portfolio™ would hold 15 percent to 35 percent of its equity exposure in international asset class funds.

VALUE VS. GROWTH

It is worth noting that the composition of the equity asset classes has a *value* emphasis and is absent the more popular *growth* category. Value stocks are categorized as having a high book-value:market-value ratio. To many investors, selecting *value* asset classes over *growth* asset classes may seem counterintuitive. Most believe that *growth* would make more sense, especially if that is exactly what they are trying to do – *grow* their portfolios. However, the research has shown repeatedly that, over the long-term, value stocks have indeed outperformed growth stocks (not necessarily in every timeframe, but certainly over the long run). This may be because they are inherently "riskier," with high book-to-market ratios. Consequently, investors demand a higher return for this added risk.

Figure 6.5 shows how dramatic the difference in performance can be over an extended period. [17]

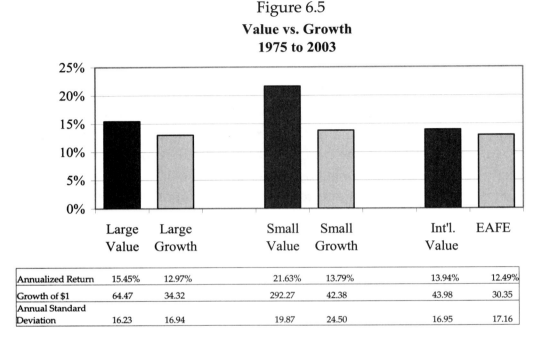

Figure 6.5

Value vs. Growth
1975 to 2003

	Large Value	Large Growth	Small Value	Small Growth	Int'l. Value	EAFE
Annualized Return	15.45%	12.97%	21.63%	13.79%	13.94%	12.49%
Growth of $1	64.47	34.32	292.27	42.38	43.98	30.35
Annual Standard Deviation	16.23	16.94	19.87	24.50	16.95	17.16

In the area of large U.S. stocks, we see a 2.48 percent difference in performance, favoring value stocks over this 29-year period. This would have resulted in nearly *twice* as much growth in actual dollars (Growth of $1). Given this huge difference, along with the fact that the risk taken (standard deviation) was only slightly higher, the value positioning offers a clear advantage. The results are similar in the area of international investing as represented by the EAFE index on the far right of the graph (1.45 percent higher for value stocks).

The most dramatic data is with the small U.S. companies in the middle columns. There was a 7.84 percent performance advantage by the small value asset class which resulted in approximately *seven times* more dollars at the end of the period. Additionally, the risk taken would have been about 19 percent *less* for the value position. *More return, less risk* – what every investor needs.

We believe this data shows that this *value positioning* is one factor responsible for the return advantage (vs. the market) we have seen exhibited by the Market Return Portfolio™ strategy over the long run. Remember however, this is still just "icing on the cake," as your goal should always be to simply get *market return with consistency.*

MORE ABOUT RISK

On a scale of risk, most investors would rank these general asset classes in the following manner: [18]

Riskiest	Emerging Markets
	Small International
	Small U.S.
	Large International
	Large U.S
	Real Estate Investment Trusts
	Long-Term Bonds.
	Intermediate Bonds
Safest	Intermediate Bonds

The MRP™ contains substantial amounts of each of these asset classes that are on all parts of the scale – including the "risky" end. It is not intuitive to think that by having a portfolio hold substantial amounts of these "riskier" asset classes it would actually have a *lower* volatility or standard deviation. But this is witness again to the miracle of *super-diversification.* Combining asset classes with different risk characteristics or dissimilar price movements actually *reduces* overall risk in a portfolio.

The risk of the whole is less than the risk of the sum of its parts.

This is one of the most important points to make about super-diversification and the MRP™ strategy.

CAN MRP™ SAVE SOCIAL SECURITY?

There is no question that the math in the Social Security equation is pretty simple. At the current pace of spending, the system is going to run out of money. It is just a matter of when. The projected date when tax receipts begin to fall short of outlays is around 2018.[19] The system is pay-as-you-go with fewer workers paying for more retirees in a society where life expectancy is now reaching into the eighties. Furthermore, there is no trust fund from which to draw. Increasing tax rates or decreasing benefit payments seem to be the only alternatives in a gridlocked Congress. With this in mind, chances are good that both of these solutions will be applied in the future. Investors under the age of 50 who have used their projected Social Security benefit in their retirement cashflow calculations may want to rethink this approach. In fact, they may want to disregard their Social Security benefit completely just to be safe.

For years now, politicians have floated ideas of just how to save the system. An alternative of allowing personal accounts directed by employees is one example that has received a fair amount of support in the past. That is, until the bear market timeframe of 2000 to 2002. The enthusiasm quickly waned as opponents used "risk of loss" scare tactics.

However, could the debate be reopened with a slightly different paradigm in place? When double-digit market return is there for the taking, can't our leaders see the logic of using free markets to pay for Social Security? Would there be anything wiser than using the power of capitalism to provide a social benefit for all? How can we ignore such an opportunity? After all, the South American nation of Chile figured this out some time ago with a privatized system. Surely the greatest nation in the world, with the greatest economic system ever created, can follow suit.

Time will tell whether or not our lawmakers ultimately decide to harness market return forces to benefit our citizens. Meanwhile, we had all better be prepared to take ultimate responsibility for our own financial futures. Fortunately, MRP™ is the tool that can aid all investors as they take personal responsibility for their retirement destiny outside the government retirement system.

So, can MRP™ save Social Security? Yes, if lawmakers let it, we are confident it can. However, the likelihood of that happening is very small. The responsible solution is to become an MRP™ investor!

A FEW MORE THOUGHTS ON THE MARKET RETURN PORTFOLIO™

We considered comparing the Market Return Portfolio™ strategy with a portfolio of active managers. The problem is, which ones? With the odds so stacked against finding enough active managers who can "beat the market," how can we possibly make the comparison? If we went back and used the best active manager performers over this timeframe, we still would be faced with the problems of survivorship and hindsight bias. But no one could have chosen those managers before they performed well (against the astronomical probabilities we spoke of in Chapter 5). Even if we assume that we could beat those ridiculous odds, would investors be patient enough with the randomly bad years of managers to stay around for their randomly good years? Human nature tells us this would be extremely difficult. Especially when we consider that the average investor holding period is only about three years.[20]

With MRP™, on the other hand, we did not data mine and find the best performers because the institutional asset class funds simply follow the market in the purest form. The results are what they are. There is no picking of these funds based on their past performances. The strategy affords basically one alternative – there is no choice or "pick" to make. We use Institutional Asset Class Funds, which provide market return. Period. This is why we say, "MRP™ is the last investment strategy you will ever need."

Once investors have arrived at the conclusion that market return is what they need and want, the temptation to change their portfolio in uncertain times is eliminated. We have gone from the uncertainty of what move to make next to the certainty that we will receive market return. Furthermore, we can have full confidence that as long as free markets are in place, we will receive the full return of the market. It is there for the taking.

GENERATING INCOME DURING RETIREMENT

A common question asked by retirees is: "How do we get income from our nest egg once we have retired?" A companion concern is that they do not want to be forced to sell a security when its value has dropped in order to have income for their household budget. We discussed earlier the important paradigm shifting truth that real long-term cost of life safety comes through owning stocks. Now we must figure out how to provide adequate cash flow without selling low.

The technique is quite simple actually. It is accomplished through periodic rebalancing. For example, if a retired couple has a 60/40 portfolio mix of stocks to bonds (Figure 6.6), this mix will naturally change over time as market fluctuations occur. After a few months or perhaps a year, the mix may be 65/35 because stocks have outpaced bonds. Conversely, it may be 55/45 if stocks have retreated during the time period. At any rate, the rebalancing will involve resetting the mix to the original 60/40 allocation. To accomplish this, the growing asset class is sold down to its original allocation. That cash is then reallocated into the asset class that shrunk to rebalance the portfolio (Figure 6.7). This rebalancing automatically creates a situation where the investor is selling high (from the asset class that grew) and buying low (into the asset class that fell behind.) This automation systematizes the very thing that all investors strive to do – sell high and buy low.

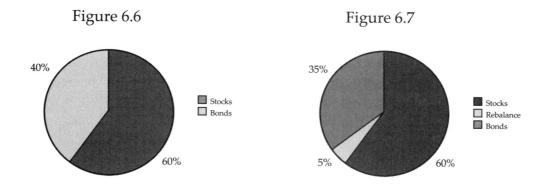

Figure 6.6   Figure 6.7

This rebalancing technique should be used in all portfolios but becomes a special advantage to a retiree. Here's how: First of all, retirees should be taking money for living expenses from the cash/fixed income side of their portfolios. Retirees should hold shorter term bonds, which have far less volatility. Naturally, when money is taken from the cash/bond side of the allocation, it reduces the percentage. When the rebalancing takes place, equities are sold in order to replenish the cash/bonds position. Consequently, a retiree is only selling the equities that are higher in order to replenish the cash/bond side. If for some reason, all stock asset classes are in an extreme bear market, then it may require holding off on the rebalancing for a short time. However, even in the deepest of recessions or bear markets, there are typically one or two stock asset classes that are not way down – perhaps flat. As long as retirees have at least four years of living expenses in the cash/bond allocation, chances are very good they can weather any market storm and have adequate cashflow through a down market without having to sell equities when they are low.

GOOD NEWS FOR TAX MANAGEMENT

Market Return Portfolio™ strategies can also be implemented on a tax-managed, tax-deferred or tax-deductible basis.

For taxable accounts, there are Institutional Asset Class Funds available that are specifically designed to minimize taxes. These tax-managed funds deliver the same consistent exposure to their asset classes but with a special emphasis on maximizing after-tax returns. These tax-efficient funds seek to offset capital gains and losses. Equity funds generate dividends that traditional management tends to ignore. This is especially true among small cap and value stocks that distribute more income than large cap growth stocks. These tax-managed strategies simultaneously attempt to minimize taxable gains and dividend yield without sacrificing precise asset class exposure and super-diversification.

On the tax-deferred side of the equation, if you have reached the maximum in funding your qualified retirement plan and have a need for additional tax deferral in your financial plan, it may make sense for a portion of your portfolio to be placed in a tax-deferred variable annuity. On the other hand, you may have already been sold a retail variable annuity and you are looking to get out from under the excessive fees that typically exist in them without also incurring income tax and penalties. In both cases, asset class funds are available within institutional variable annuities. In addition, the mortality and expense charges associated with institutional annuities are considerably less than their retail counterparts.

Finally, tax-qualified plans that allow tax deductions, such as IRAs, pension plans and the popular 401(k), are also eligible to hold Institutional Asset Class Funds. This allows implementation of an MRP™ strategy for retirement plans as well.

FIVE STEPS TO WEALTH WITHOUT WORRY:

The following is designed to give investors a simple, usable list of what to do now. At the completion of these five steps, you are on your way to changing your financial life forever.

1. Get the right help. Find a qualified advisor based on the questions and guidelines set forth in Chapter 4. An independent, direct pay, market return advisor will be the gateway to the Institutional Asset Class Funds that will allow you to access the market return that is *there for the taking* in the MRP™ strategy.

2. **Create an *Investment Policy Statement*.** This written document allows you and your advisor to create a long-term strategy based on historic data and your specific goals and needs; *not* emotion. Whenever you become a little tense about markets, reviewing the IPS allows you to regain your confidence in the free market system and reminds you why you made previous prudent decisions to allocate your investments in a certain way. It also allows you the comfort of staying in the market for the long haul.

3. **Diversify and own them *all*.** The best time to super-diversify is always *right now*. If you have company stock in a 401(k) or think you are well diversified simply because you have numerous individual securities or mutual funds, look closely. You don't want to make a costly mistake – especially now that you know better. Rely on the miracle of capitalism. If you have been paralyzed with indecision because of market fluctuations, get in the market now. The best place for long-term investment dollars (5+ years) is in the market. Hesitation smells of timing – not time *in*. Now that stock selection is a non-factor, you can own markets (not just stocks) and capture the capital market return that belongs to *every* investor – including you! This will allow free markets to work for you while you work (or play) at something else.

4. **Stop watching markets.** By allowing markets to do the work, you can eliminate the time-consuming stressful activity of watching market ups and downs. This in turn allows you to avoid emotional mistakes that often accompany market-watching activity. Now that you understand that *timing* and *picking* decisions are futile anyway, what's the point?

5. **Do something worthwhile.** Look at all the time and energy that has now been freed up for really important things! Never again should you be a slave to market or economic news. This affords a great opportunity to reevaluate the things in life that are important to you and your family. It is time to get a new hobby, spend more time with loved ones or get involved with a worthy cause.

Conclusion

In the *Introduction* of this book, we stated that you may be asking questions such as: "Why haven't I heard of this before?" and "Why isn't everyone doing this?" We are *still* asking those same questions. Particularly when we consider that the fundamental principles of the MRP™ strategy, which are derived directly from *Modern Portfolio Theory,* have been taught in business schools around the country for decades. The following are a few answers we've found:

- The media thrives on "newsworthy" market volatility and uncertainty, which fosters active management habits among investors. Good market news and a *market return* strategy is considered "boring."
- Major brokerage houses and financial firms are not in the business of educating the public. They *are* in the business of marketing *products* to the public.
- The politics and organizational structure of the financial services delivery system makes the dissemination and acceptance of MRP™ principles on a mass scale almost impossible. As Descartes once said, "A man is incapable of comprehending any argument that interferes with his revenue."

It is our sincerest hope that our message of simplicity, efficiency and logic has helped you see the advantages of the Market Return Portfolio™ strategy. It is intended to deliver market return with market risk – and that only. There are no empty promises of "beating the market" or "getting rich quick."

The MRP™ strategy is simply the best way to invest and thus benefit from the capitalist system that has made our country great. We hope you have seen that this is genuinely *the last investment strategy you will ever need*. We know that you can now enjoy the peace of mind that comes from doing the right thing with your money. We expect to hear of your great accomplishments as you create wealth without worry – now that you know it is *There for the Taking!*

"A mind once stretched by a new idea never returns to its old dimensions."
–Oliver Wendell Holmes

Notes

Chapter 1

1. "Privileged Information from Peter Lynch, The Biggest Mistakes to Avoid Now," *The Bottom Line,* March 1, 1994.
2. Burton Malkiel, *A Random Walk Down Wall Street* (New York, W.W. Norton, 1996), p. 186.
3. http://www.twainquotes.com/Lies.html. As noted at this Web site, it is unlikely that this was actually said by Disraeli. The quote "There are three kinds of lies: lies, damned lies and statistics." is more likely from Leonard Courtney.
4. David Dreman, *Contrarian Investment Strategy: The Psychology of Stock Market Success* (New York, Random House, 1979).
5. Remarks by Federal Reserve Chairman Alan Greenspan at the Annual Dinner and Francis Boyer Lecture of The American Enterprise Institute for Public Policy Research. Mr. Greenspan's speech was titled "The Challenge of Central Banking in a Democratic Society."
http://www.federalreserve.gov/boarddocs/speeches/1996/19961205.htm
6. Dimensional Fund Advisors
7. Morningstar Principia Pro Database, December 2003. Includes only mutual funds with 85 percent or more in U.S. equity holdings, excluding index funds and funds that do not have an Annualized 10-year return. Distinct portfolios only.
8. Ibid.

Chapter 2

1. We categorized a *bear* market as a 20 percent or more drop in the S&P 500 Index. From 1926 to 2003 there have been 13 bear markets.

Time Period	S&P 500
9-29 to 11-29	-33.08%
4-30 to 6-32	-79.570%
8-32 to 2-33	-29.82%
2-34 to 6-34	-20.70%
3-37 to 3-38	-50.04%
10-39 to 5-40	-25.72%
9-41 to 4-42	-22.39%
6-46 to 4-47	-20.96%
1-62 to 6-62	-22.28%
12-68 to 6-70	-29.23%
1-73 to 9-74	-42.62%
9-87 to 11-87	-29.53%
9-00 to 9-02	-44.73%

Bull (non-bear) market periods for the S&P 500 Index from 1926 to 2003:

Time Period	S&P 500
1-26 to 8-29	193.29%
12-29 to 3-30	21.40%
7-32 to 8-32	91.60%
3-33 to 1-34	105.35%
8-34 to 2-37	135.14%
4-38 to 9-39	64.68%
6-40 to 8-41	20.95%
5-42 to 5-46	209.84%
5-47 to 12-61	925.44%
7-62 to 11-68	143.85%
7-70 to 12-72	75.60%
10-74 to 8-87	843.64%
12-87 to 8-00	814.15%
10-02 to 12-03	39.54%

2. David Rynecki, "Ten Stocks to Last a Decade," *Fortune*, August 14, 2000.
3. Does not include dividends.

4. Marion Asnes, Peter Carbonara, et al, "Money 100 – The Best 100 Mutual Funds, The Only List You Need," Money, June 1999.
5. Data Source: Morningstar Principia Pro Database, December 2003 and CNN Money.
6. Funds A, B, C and D are actual funds. They are not identified because the purpose of this illustration is not to sell a particular security. It is to emphasize that ratings, in and of themselves, do not provide enough information for making an investment decision. Funds were analyzed in December 2000 and January 2001. Source: Dimensional Fund Advisors.
7. Paul Asquith, Michael Mikhail, and Andrea Ai, "The Information in Equity Analyst Reports." National Bureau of Economic Research. http://www.nber.org/digest/apr03/w9246.html.
8. Berkshire Hathaway 2004 Annual Report, pp. 2, 5.
9. Morningstar Principia Database, December 2003.
10. Morningstar Principia Pro Database, December 2003. Includes only mutual funds with 85 percent or more in U.S. equity holdings and that fall within the "large" portion of Morningstar's style box. Excludes index funds and those that do not have a 10-year annualized return. Distinct portfolios only.
11. Performance noted does not include dividends.
12. The Equity Market Return Portfolio™ is comprised of funds managed by Dimensional Fund Advisors (DFA). The composition of the portfolio is detailed below:

Equity Portfolio	Percentage
DFA Enhanced U.S. Large Company	20%
DFA U.S. Large Cap Value	20%
DFA U.S. Micro Cap	10%
DFA U.S. Small Cap Value	10%
DFA Real Estate Securities	10%
DFA International Value	10%
DFA International Small Company	5%
DFA International Small Cap Value	5%
DFA Emerging Markets	3%
DFA Emerging Markets Value	3%
DFA Emerging Markets Small Cap	4%

See Appendix A for additional portfolio composition information.

13. Ian McDonald, "Mutual-Fund Expenses Keep Rising – Despite Trading Probes, Firms Post Better Profits, Helped by Increasing Fees," *Wall Street Journal Online*, November 3, 2003.
14. Morningstar Principia Pro Database, December 2003. Selection criteria includes only Dimensional Fund Advisor funds.

Chapter 3

1. See Appendix B
2. Arthur Levitt, *Take on the Street* (New York, Pantheon, 2002), p. 56.
3. U.S. Securities and Exchange Commission, Division of Investment Management: Report on Mutual Fund Fees and Expenses, December 2000. http://www.sec.gov/news/studies/feestudy.htm
   Carhart, Mark M., 1997, *On Persistence in Mutual Fund Performance*, Journal of Finance 52, 57–82.
4. Morningstar Principia Pro Database, December 2003. Includes only mutual funds with 85 percent or more in U.S. equity holdings, excluding index funds and DFA funds. Distinct portfolios only.
5. Morningstar Principia Pro Database as of March 31, 2004.
6. Yuka Hayash, "Funds Closed at Brisk Pace in 2003," *Wall Street Journal Online*, March 4, 2004.
7. Includes funds having minimum assets of $100m at the end of 1996 (851 funds).
8. For example, the NBA Eastern Conference franchises had replaced 14 of 15 head coaches halfway through the season in 2003-2004.
9. Morningstar Principia Pro Database, December 2003. Includes only mutual funds with 85 percent or more in U.S. equity holdings, excluding index funds and DFA funds. Distinct portfolios only.
10. The fund being described is the Fidelity Magellan Fund.
11. Einstein was quoting Benjamin Franklin.

Chapter 4

1. Senator Carter Glass (D-Va.) and Congressman Henry Steagall (D-Ala.) introduced legislation in 1933, in the midst of the Depression, that sought to separate commercial banking and securities underwriting (brokerage services). The law eventually became known as the Glass-Steagall Act of

1933. It was designed to prevent the conflicts of interests that supposedly arose when commercial banks provided banking and investment services to the public. Additional limits on the activities of banks and bank holding companies were enacted in 1956 with the passage of the Bank Holding Company Act. Under this Act banks and bank holding companies were prevented from offering non-banking services such as providing insurance. This legislation was an effort to control the growing trend toward financial services conglomerates. In April of 1998, 65 years after the passage of Glass-Steagall, Travelers Corporation and Citicorp announced the world's largest merger – today's Citigroup. At the time the two companies provided services that included banking, brokerage and insurance. Congress paved the way for this merger 18 months later with the passage of the Financial Services Modernization Act of 1999, effectively repealing Glass-Steagall. http://www.sia.com/capitol_hill/html/glass-steagall_act.html and http://banking.senate.gov/conf/somfinal.htm

2. Daniel Solin, *Does Your Broker Owe You Money?* (Indianapolis, Alpha, 2003), p. 232.
3. Arthur Levitt, *Take on the Street,* (New York, Pantheon, 2002), p. 312,
4. http://www.brainyquote.com/quotes/authors/v/vernon_law.html
5. Thomas Spinelli and Margaret Honan, "Recruiting Pressures Grow," *The National Underwriter Company*, March 22, 2004.

Chapter 5

1. Interest rates were taken from February 1980 and February 2000. Inflation CPI Data Source: Dimensional Fund Advisors. http://research.stlouisfed.org/fred2/data/TB1YA.txt
2. S&P 500 Index represents large cap stocks. CRSP (Center for Research in Securities Pricing, University of Chicago) deciles 6-10 represent small cap stocks.
3. Weston Wellington, "Lessons of 2003," Dimensional Fund Advisors, March 2004. http://my.dfaus.com.
4. S&P 500 represents large cap stocks. The CRSP deciles 9-10 represent small cap stocks. International stocks are represented by the MSCI EAFE (Morgan Stanley Capital International Europe Australia and the Far East).

5. Morningstar Principia Database, December 2003. The universe of funds was filtered as described below:

   (a) Large growth funds – includes stock funds with 85 percent or more in U.S. companies that fall in Morningstar's "large growth" category. Excludes index funds, enhanced index funds and DFA funds. Distinct portfolio only. Large growth funds were compared against the Russell 1000 Growth Index.

   (b) Large value funds – includes stock funds with 85 percent or more in U.S. companies that fall in Morningstar's "large value" category. Excludes index funds, enhanced index funds and DFA funds. Distinct portfolio only. Large value funds were compared against the Russell 1000 Value Index.

   (c) Small value funds – includes stock funds with 85 percent or more in U.S. companies that fall in Morningstar's "small value" category. Excludes index funds, enhanced index funds and DFA funds. Distinct portfolio only. Small value funds were compared against the Russell 2000 Value Index.

   (d) International funds – includes stock funds that fall in Morningstar's prospectus objective as "foreign stock" and falls into Morningstar's style box as "large cap." Excludes index funds, enhanced index funds and DFA funds. Distinct portfolio only. International funds were compared against the MSCI EAFE Index.

6. Bud Carter, "Chairman Carter's Collection of Pithy Quotes," 2003, p. 19.

7. See note 5. Beta filter equal to or less than 1.0 was added to previous category filters.

8. The Equity, Aggressive, and Balanced *Market Return Portfolios*™ are comprised of funds managed by Dimensional Fund Advisors. The composition of the portfolios are detailed below:

Equity Portfolio	Percentage
DFA Enhanced U.S. Large Company	20%
DFA U.S. Large Cap Value	20%
DFA U.S. Micro Cap	10%
DFA U.S. Small Cap Value	10%
DFA Real Estate Securities	10%
DFA International Value	10%

Equity Portfolio	Percentage
DFA International Small Company	5%
DFA International Small Cap Value	5%
DFA Emerging Markets	3%
DFA Emerging Markets Value	3%
DFA Emerging Markets Small Cap	4%

Aggressive Portfolio	Percentage
DFA Enhanced U.S. Large Company	16%
DFA U.S. Large Cap Value	16%
DFA U.S. Micro Cap	8%
DFA U.S. Small Cap Value	8%
DFA Real Estate Securities	8%
DFA International Value	8%
DFA International Small Company	4%
DFA International Small Cap Value	4%
DFA Emerging Markets	2.4%
DFA Emerging Markets Value	2.4%
DFA Emerging Markets Small Cap	3.2%
DFA One-Year Fixed Income	5%
DFA Two-Year Global Fixed Income	5%
DFA Five-Year Government	5%
DFA Five-Year Global Fixed Income	5%

Balanced Portfolio	Percentage
DFA Enhanced U.S. Large Company	12%
DFA U.S. Large Cap Value	12%
DFA U.S. Micro Cap	6%
DFA U.S. Small Cap Value	6%
DFA Real Estate Securities	6%
DFA International Value	6%
DFA International Small Company	3%
DFA International Small Cap Value	3%
DFA Emerging Markets	1.8%

DFA Emerging Markets Value	1.8%
DFA Emerging Markets Small Cap	2.4%
DFA One-Year Fixed Income	10%
DFA Two-Year Global Fixed Income	10%
DFA Five-Year Government	10%
DFA Five-Year Global Fixed Income	10%

See Appendix A for additional portfolio composition information.

9. Ibid.
10. Ibid.
11. Morningstar Principia Database, December 2003. The universe of funds was filtered as described below:
   (a) Large Cap funds – includes stock funds with 85 percent or more in U.S. companies that fall in Morningstar's "large" style box. Excludes index funds, enhanced index funds, DFA funds and funds that did not have year 2000 returns. Distinct portfolio only; 876 funds.
   (b) Mid Cap Funds – includes stock funds with 85 percent or more in U.S. companies that fall in Morningstar's "mid cap" style box. Excludes index funds, enhanced index funds, DFA funds and funds that did not have year 2000 returns. Distinct portfolio only; 375 funds.
   (c) Small Cap funds – includes stock funds with 85 percent or more in U.S. companies that fall in Morningstar's "small" style box. Excludes index funds, enhanced index funds, DFA funds and funds that did not have year 2000 returns. Distinct portfolio only; 348 funds.
   A scheduled portfolio was prepared in Morningstar Principia Pro for each of the above categories using a timeframe of March 1, 2000 to December 31, 2003. With a total of 1,387 funds used, a weighted return was applied to each category and then summarized.
12. See note 8.

Chapter 6

1. *The Bible*, Matthew 7:24-27.
2. http://www.holland.nl/uk/holland/sights/tulips-history.html.
3. Harry Markowitz, "Portfolio Selection," *The Journal of Finance*, March 1952, pp. 77-91.

His work was first published while he was still in graduate school at the University of Chicago. Markowitz proposed that you could build a diversified portfolio that would lower risk as well as provide higher returns because of the benefits of diversification. According to his theory, investors can build optimal portfolios that maximize expected return for any level of market risk. The research in portfolio construction that has evolved from the 1952 paper by Markowitz is known as Modern Portfolio Theory.

4. Discussion of institutional asset class fund characteristics derived from more detailed discussion on pages 70-76 in *The Prudent Investor's Guide to Beating Wall Street at Its Own Game*, John J. Bowen & Daniel C. Goldie. McGraw-Hill, New York, 1998.

5. Institutional asset class funds are traditional open-ended mutual funds. Open-ended mutual fund investors can purchase or sell shares during trading hours and receive that evening's closing price. Cash from the sale of a mutual fund is made available upon settlement of the trade based on Federal Reserve guidelines.

6. See Chapter 2, Note 9.

7. See Chapter 2, Note 10.

8. See Chapter 3, Note 6.

9. The fund management team uses objective criteria based on academic research. For example, in the small U.S. company category, small companies are defined as those whose market capitalization (price x shares outstanding) comprises the smallest, 12.5 percent, of the total market universe. The total market universe is defined as the aggregate capitalization of the NYSE, AMEX and NASDAQ National Market System companies. They also employ additional screening criteria. These criteria include eliminating REITs, closed-end investment companies, limited partnerships, companies in bankruptcy, ADRs, companies with qualified financial statements, OTC stocks with fewer than four market makers and those not included on the National Market System. They are aggressive in keeping cash levels low, generally under 2 percent. New cashflow is controlled so portfolios may remain fully invested. On at least a semiannual basis, the market capitalization ranking of eligible stocks is examined to determine which issues are eligible for purchase and which are sale candidates. A hold or buffer range for sales minimizes transaction

costs and keeps portfolio turnover low. Issues that migrate above the hold range are sold and proceeds reinvested in the portfolio.

10. See Chapter 2, Note 10.

11. Gary Brinson, Randolph Hood and Gilbert Beebower, "Determinants of Portfolio Performance," *Financial Analyst Journal*, July-August 1986, pp. 39-44.

12. The Diversified Index Portfolio (DIP) is an 80:20 stock to bond ratio. S&P 500 Index represents large cap stocks; Russell 2000 Index represents small cap stocks; MSCI EAFE Index represents international stocks; Lehman Brother Intermediate Government/Credit Index represents fixed income holdings.

13. The 80:20 Market Return Portfolio™ is comprised of funds managed by Dimensional Fund Advisors. The composition of the portfolio is detailed below:

80:20 Portfolio	Percentage
DFA Enhanced U.S. Large Company	16%
DFA U.S. Large Cap Value	16%
DFA U.S. Micro Cap	8%
DFA U.S. Small Cap Value	8%
DFA Real Estate Securities	8%
DFA International Value	8%
DFA International Small Company	4%
DFA International Small Cap Value	4%
DFA Emerging Markets	2.4%
DFA Emerging Markets Value	2.4%
DFA Emerging Markets Small Cap	3.2%
DFA One-Year Fixed Income	5%
DFA Two-Year Global Fixed Income	5%
DFA Five-Year Government	5%
DFA Five-Year Global Fixed Income	5%

See Appendix A for additional portfolio composition information.

14. Number of holdings is as of March 31, 2004.

Portfolio Fund Name	# of Holdings
DFA U.S. Large Cap Value	212
DFA U.S. Micro Cap	2693
DFA U.S. Small Cap Value	1505
DFA Real Estate Securities	129
DFA International Value	671
DFA International Small Company	3,994
DFA International Small Cap Value	2,473
DFA Emerging Markets	518
DFA Emerging Markets Value	1,224
DFA Emerging Markets Small Cap	1,250

Index Name	# of Holdings
S&P 500 Index	500
Russell 2000 Index	1,932
MSCI EAFE Index	1,000

15. John Bowen and Daniel Goldie, *The Prudent Investor's Guide to Beating Wall Street at Its Own Game*, (New York, McGraw-Hill, 1998), p. 99.
Bowen and Goldie cite as an example the returns of Colgate-Palmolive, Inc., which receives "about 80 percent of its revenues from foreign operations, yet its stock price still closely followed the U.S. market during a period when foreign markets significantly underperformed [1992-1997]. Because stocks of U.S. multinational firms are so highly correlated with the U.S. market, they lose their diversification power. To capture the diversification benefits of foreign equities, you must purchase shares of companies headquartered in foreign countries."

16. Annualized returns. Data Source: Dimensional Fund Advisors Matrix Book 2004.

Index Name	Return
S&P 500	17.9%
Japan Large Cap	36.1%
Global Large Cap	25.4%

17. Large Cap and Small Cap Indices are from Fama/French data. Eugene Fama University of Chicago; Kenneth French MIT. EAFE is Morgan Stanley Capital International Europe, Australia, and the Far East Index. Data Source: Dimensional Fund Advisors.

18. Rankings are based on standard deviation. Data Source: Dimensional Fund Advisors.

19. http://www.ssa.gov/OACT/TRSUM/trsummary.html.

20. Transcript of John Bogle statement before the United States Senate Committee on Banking, Housing, and Urban Affairs, February 26, 2004, p. 9.

Appendix A

Series include simulated and live returns. For portfolio construction, simulated data is used prior to the inception of the live portfolio. Simulated data does not reflect deduction of advisory fees, brokerage fees and other expenses that a client would pay. Nor do simulated returns represent results of actual trading. Notations that follow identify which periods are simulated and which periods contain live data for each data series. Live data does not reflect the deduction of advisory fees, brokerage fees and other expenses incurred by the portfolios. Live data incorporates actual trading results. Both simulated and live data reflect total returns.

Large Cap Market weighting allocated to US Large Company Portfolio prior to August 1996 and allocated to S&P 500 Index prior to January 1991. Real Estate Stocks weighting allocated evenly between US Micro Cap Portfolio and US Small Cap Value Portfolio prior to January 1975 data inception. International Large Cap Value weighting allocated evenly between International Small Company Portfolio and MSCI EAFE Index (net dividends) prior to January 1975 data inception. International Small Cap weighting allocated to International Small Company Portfolio prior to January 1995 data inception. Emerging Markets Large, Value, and Small weighting allocated evenly between International Value Portfolio and International Small Company Portfolio prior to data inception January 1987. Five-Year Global Fixed Income Portfolio weighting allocated evenly between One-Year Fixed Income Portfolio, Two-Year Global Fixed Income Portfolio, and Five-Year Government Portfolio prior to January 1987 data inception.

U.S. Equities

U.S. MICRO CAP STOCKS
1926-1981: Deciles 9-10 NYSE[1](plus AMEX[2] equivalents since July 1962 and NASDAQ[3] equivalents since 1973). Courtesy of CRSP[4]. 1982-2003: U.S. Micro Cap Portfolio net of all fees.

U.S. SMALL CAP STOCKS
1926-May 1986: Deciles 6-10 NYSE (plus AMEX equivalents since July 1962 and NASDAQ equivalents since 1973). Courtesy of CRSP. June 1986-2003: U.S Small Cap Trust net of administrative fees.

S&P 500 INDEX
© *Stocks, Bond, Bills, and Inflation 2003* Yearbook™, Ibbotson Associates, Chicago (annually updated work by Roger G. Ibbotson and Rex A. Sinquefield). Used with permission. All rights reserved.

U.S. SMALL CAP VALUE STOCKS
1927-February 1992: Simulated strategy of lower-half market cap, upper 30 percent book-to-market NYSE (plus AMEX equivalents since July 1962 and NASDAQ equivalents since 1973). Courtesy of Fama/French and CRSP. March 1992-2003: U.S Small Cap Value Trust net of administrative fees.

U.S. LARGE CAP VALUE STOCKS
1927-March 1993: Simulated strategy of upper-half market cap, upper 30 percent book-to-market NYSE (plus AMEX equivalents since July 1962 and NASDAQ equivalents since 1973). Courtesy of Fama/French and CRSP. Excludes utilities. April 1993-2003: U.S Large Value Portfolio net of all fees.

U.S. SMALL CAP GROWTH STOCKS
Simulated strategy of lower-half market cap, lower 30 percent book-to-market NYSE (plus AMEX equivalents since July 1962 and NASDAQ equivalents since 1973). Courtesy of Fama/French and CRSP.

U.S. LARGE CAP GROWTH STOCKS
Simulated strategy of upper-half market cap, lower 30 percent book-to-market NYSE (plus AMEX equivalents since July 1962 and NASDAQ equivalents since 1973). Courtesy of Fama/French and CRSP. Excludes utilities.

U.S. EQUITY REAL ESTATE INVESTMENT TRUSTS

1975-November 1994: Courtesy of Professor Donald Keim, Wharton School. Excludes healthcare REITs. December 1994-2003: Real Estate Securities Portfolio net of all fees.

U.S. SMALL CAP PORTFOLIO

1973-March 1992: Deciles 6-10 NYSE (plus AMEX equivalents since July 1962 and NASDAQ equivalents since 1973). Courtesy of CRSP. April 1992-2003: U.S. Small Cap Portfolio net of all fees.

U.S. SMALL CAP VALUE PORTFOLIO

1973-March 1993: Simulated strategy of lower-half market cap, upper 30 percent book-to-market NYSE (plus AMEX and NASDAQ equivalents). Courtesy of Fama/French and CRSP. Excludes utilities. April 1993-2001: U.S. Small Cap Value Portfolio net of all fees. Excludes utilities.

U.S. LARGE COMPANY PORTFOLIO

1973-1990: S&P 500 Index. 1991-2003: U.S. large company portfolio net of all fees.

ENHANCED U.S. LARGE COMPANY PORTFOLIO

Enhanced U.S. Large Company Portfolio net of all fees.

Fixed Income

LONG-TERM GOVERNMENT BONDS

Average maturity: 20 years. © Stocks, Bonds, Bills, and Inflations 2003 Yearbook™, Ibbotson Associates, Chicago (annually updated work by Roger G. Ibbotson and Rex A. Sinquefield). Used with permission. All rights reserved.

LONG-TERM CORPORATE BONDS

Average maturity: 20 years. © Stocks, Bonds, Bills, and Inflations 2003 Yearbook™, Ibbotson Associates, Chicago (annually updated work by Roger G. Ibbotson and Rex A. Sinquefield). Used with permission. All rights reserved.

ONE-MONTH TREASURY BILLS

Average maturity: 30 days © Stocks, Bonds, Bills, and Inflations 2003 Yearbook™, Ibbotson Associates, Chicago (annually updated work by Roger G. Ibbotson and Rex A. Sinquefield). Used with permission. All rights reserved.

ONE-MONTH CERTIFICATES OF DEPOSIT

1947-1971: One-month banker' acceptances. 1972-2003: One-month certificates of deposit.

ONE-YEAR FIXED INCOME STRATEGY

Average maturity: Less than one year. 1972-July 1983: Simulated CD fixed income strategy (maximum maturity one year). August 1983-2003: One-Year Fixed Income Portfolio net of all fees.

FIVE-YEAR GOVERNMENT STRATEGY

Average maturity: Less than five years. 1953-May 1987: Stimulation using U.S. government instruments (maximum maturity five years). June 1987-2003: Five-Year Government Portfolio net of all fees.

LEHMAN BROTHERS INTERMEDIATE GOVERNMENT/CREDIT BOND INDEX

Weighted average maturity 3.5 - 4.5 years. Courtesy of Lehman Brothers, Inc.

TWO-YEAR GLOBAL FIXED INCOME PORTFOLIO

Average maturity: Two years or Less 1973-February 1996: Simulation using U.S. government instruments (maximum maturity two years). March 1996-2003: Two-Year Global Income Portfolio net of all fees.

FIVE-YEAR GLOBAL FIXED INCOME PORTFOLIO

Average maturity: Five Years or less. 1987-November 1990: Lehman Hedged Country Indices: Equally-weighted. U.S., U.K., Australia, Canada, Germany, France, Japan, Netherlands. Courtesy of Lehman Brothers, Inc. December 1990-2003: Five-Year Global Fixed Income Portfolio net of all fees.

International Equities

INTERNATIONAL SMALL CAP STOCKS AND INTERNATIONAL LARGE CAP STOCKS (COUNTRY WEIGHTS SAME FOR BOTH STRATEGIES)

1970-June 1988: 50 percent Japan, 50 percent United Kingdom. July 1988-September 1989: 50 percent Japan, 30 percent Continental, 20 percent United Kingdom. October 1989-March 1990: 40 percent Japan, 30 percent Continental, 20 percent United Kingdom, 10 percent Pacific Rim. April 1990-1992: 40 percent Japan, 35 percent Continental, 15 percent United Kingdom, 10 percent Pacific Rim. 1993-March 1997: 35 percent Japan, 35 percent Continental, 15 percent United Kingdom, 15 percent Pacific Rim. April 1997-March 1998: 30 percent Japan, 35 percent Continental, 15 percent United Kingdom, 20 percent Pacific Rim. April 1998-August 2000: 25 percent Japan, 40 percent Continental, 20 percent United Kingdom, 15 percent Pacific Rim. September 2000-March 2002: 35 percent Japan, 35 percent Continental, 15 percent United Kingdom, 15 percent Pacific Rim. April 2002-October 2003: 29 percent Japan, 42 percent Continental, 15 percent United Kingdom, 14 percent Pacific Rim. November 2003-Decemner 2003: 27 percent Japan, 40 percent Continental, 20 percent United Kingdom, 13 percent Pacific Rim. November 2003-December 2003: 27 percent Japan, 40 percent Continental, 20 percent United Kingdom, 13 percent Pacific Rim.

GLOBAL SMALL CAP STOCKS

1970-1986: 50 percent U.S. small cap stocks, 50 percent international small cap stocks. 1987-2003: 50 percent U.S. small cap stocks, 42.5 percent international small cap stocks, 7.5 percent emerging markets small cap stocks

GLOBAL LARGE CAP STOCKS

1970-1986:50 percent S&P Index, 50 percent international large cap stocks. 1987-2003:50 percent S&P 500 Index, 42.5 percent international large cap stocks, 7.5 percent emerging markets stocks.

JAPAN SMALL CAP STOCKS

1970-March 1986: Smaller half of first section, Tokyo Stock Exchange. Courtesy of the Nomura Securities Investment Trust Management Company, Ltd., Tokyo, rebalanced semiannually. April 1986-2003: Japanese small company portfolio net of all fees.

JAPAN LARGE CAP STOCKS

1970-June 1986: Larger half of first section, Tokyo Stock Exchange. Courtesy of the Nomura Securities Investment Trust Management Company Ltd., Tokyo. July 1986-2003: Japan Index, gross dividends reinvested (in U.S. Dollars). Courtesy of Morgan Stanley Capital International.

UNITED KINGDOM SMALL CAP STOCKS

1956-March 1986: Hoare Govett Smaller Companies Index. Courtesy London School of Business. April 1986-2003: United Kingdom Small Company Portfolio net of all fees.

UNITED KINGDOM LARGE CAP STOCKS

FTSE All-Shares Index. Courtesy of FTSE.

CONTINENTAL SMALL CAP STOCKS

Countries presently include: Austria, Belgium, Denmark, Finland, France, Germany, Greece, Ireland, Italy, the Netherlands, Norway, Portugal, Spain, Sweden and Switzerland. Continental Small Company Portfolio net of all fees.

CONTINENTAL LARGE CAP STOCKS

Europe excluding United Kingdom Index, gross dividends reinvested (in U.S. Dollars). Courtesy of Morgan Stanley Capital International.

PACIFIC RIM SMALL CAP STOCKS

Countries presently include: Australia, Hong Kong, New Zealand and Singapore. October 1989-1992: Pacific Rim Small Company Trust net of administrative fees. 1993-2003: Pacific Rim Small Company Portfolio net of all fees.

PACIFIC RIM LARGE CAP STOCKS

Pacific Rim excluding Japan Index, gross dividends reinvested (in U.S. Dollars). Courtesy of Morgan Stanley Capital International.

MSCI EAFE INDEX

Europe, Australia and Far East Index. Courtesy of Morgan Stanley Capital International. Net dividends.

INTERNATIONAL VALUE STOCKS

1975-March 1993: Simulated value-weighted, unhedged strategy of stocks in Japan (maximum weight 38 percent), United Kingdom, Germany, France, the Netherlands, Belgium, Italy, Switzerland, Australia and Hong Kong with over $500 million market cap and upper 30 percent book-to-market, returns in dollars. Courtesy of Fama/French. April 1993-June 1993: MSCI EAFE Index substituted temporarily due to data availability. July 1993-February 1994: International High Book-to-Market Portfolio net of all fees. March 1994-2003: International Value Portfolio net of all fees.

EMERGING MARKETS SMALL CAP STOCKS

Countries presently include: Argentina, Brazil, Hungary, Indonesia, Israel, Malaysia, Mexico, Philippines, Poland, South Korea, Taiwan, Thailand and Turkey. Equally-weighted, rebalanced monthly. 1987-1996: Courtesy of Fama/French ("Value versus Growth: The International Evidence.") Journal of Finance 53 (1998), 1975-99.). 1997-February 1998- Emerging Markets Small Cap Series net of all fees. March 1998-2003: Emerging Markets Small Cap Portfolio net of all fees.

EMERGING MARKETS STOCKS

Chile if also included in the emerging markets strategy. 1987-February 1993: Courtesy of Fama/French ("Value versus Growth: The International Evidence" Journal of Finance 53 (1998), 1975-99.) March 1993-May 1994: Emerging Markets Closed-End Portfolio net of all fees. June 1994-2003: Emerging Markets Open-End Portfolio net of all fees.

EMERGING MARKETS VALUE STOCKS

Chile is also included in the emerging markets value strategy. 1987-February 1993: Courtesy of Fama/French ("Value versus Growth: The International Evidence." Journal of Finance 53 (1998), 1975-99.) March 1993-May 1994: Emerging Markets Closed-End Portfolio net of all fees. June 1994-March 1998: Emerging Markets Value Fund Inc. April 1998-2003: Emerging Markets Value Portfolio of all fees.

INTERNATIONAL SMALL COMPANY PROTFOLIO

1970-September 1996: International small cap stocks. October 1996-2003: International Small Company Portfolio net of all fees.

INTERNATIONAL SMALL CAP VALUE PORTFOLIO

International Small Cap Value Portfolio net of all fees.

INTERNATIONAL LARGE CAP PORTFOLIO

1973-July 1991: MSCI EAFE Index (net dividends). August 1991-2003: International Large Cap Portfolio net of all fees.

Inflation

INFLATION: CHANGES IN THE CONSUMER PRICE INDEX

© *Stocks, Bonds, Bills, and Inflation 2003 Yearbook™*, Ibbotson Associates, Chicago (annually updated work buy Roger G. Ibbotson and Rex A. Sinquefield). Used with permission. All rights reserved.

[1] NYSE: New York Stock Exchange

[2] AMEX: American Stock Exchange

[3] NASDAQ: NASDAQ National Market System

[4] CRSP: Center for Research in Security Prices, University of Chicago

Appendix A Source: Dimensional Fund Advisors Matrix Book 2003.

B

Appendix B

Year	F/F Lrg Val Index	F/F Lrg Co. Index	F/F Lrg Gro Index	F/F Sml Val Index	F/F Sml Co. Index	F/F Sml Gro Index	One Month T-Bills	5-Year T Notes	Long Term Gov't Bonds	Long Term Corp. Bonds
1927	31.25	22.93	46.18	35.29	25	31.42	3.13	4.51	8.94	7.44
1928	23.63	31.87	48.05	40.96	39.64	34.86	3.23	0.92	0.08	2.84
1929	-3.93	0.27	-21.07	-35.77	-30.78	-44.23	4.74	6.02	3.42	3.27
1930	-43.16	-29.32	-26.44	-46.38	-31.23	-35.85	2.43	6.72	4.65	7.98
1931	-58.24	-60.13	-36.96	-51.87	-47.4	-42.7	1.09	-2.31	-5.32	-1.85
1932	-3.26	-15.61	-7.93	1.35	-10.26	-5.25	0.95	8.81	16.84	10.82
1933	116.91	90.03	44.65	118.69	125.63	159.41	0.3	1.83	-0.07	10.38
1934	-21.51	-3.25	11.06	8.51	18.25	35.89	0.18	9	10.01	13.84
1935	51.14	47.15	42.22	53.16	76.69	48.34	0.14	6.99	5	9.61
1936	48.12	38.25	26.46	73.19	48.92	37.1	0.19	3.04	7.5	6.74
1937	-41.07	-31.91	-34.12	-51.47	-48.74	-48.64	0.29	1.57	0.22	2.75
1938	25.2	20.04	33.2	26.21	43.39	43.81	-0.04	6.23	5.51	6.13
1939	-12.51	-3.22	7.73	-3.55	0.7	10.72	0.01	4.52	5.95	3.97
1940	-2.62	-2.78	-9.81	-9.83	-1.82	0.57	-0.02	2.96	6.09	3.39
1941	-0.88	-4.72	-12.67	-4.82	-10.96	-17.34	0.04	0.49	0.93	2.73
1942	33.71	17.48	13.17	35	29.2	16.76	0.28	1.92	3.22	2.6
1943	44.02	34	22.04	91.82	55.09	45.08	0.35	2.8	2.07	2.83
1944	41.98	22.27	16.11	49.71	40.12	41.23	0.33	1.81	2.82	4.73
1945	49.06	38.87	31.95	74.61	59.73	64.28	0.32	2.21	10.73	4.08
1946	-8.29	-1.41	-8.29	-7.36	-10.26	-12.4	0.36	1.01	-0.09	1.72
1947	8.66	4.25	4.1	5.34	-2.49	-8.38	0.5	0.92	-2.63	-2.34
1948	5.09	1.59	3.35	-2.3	-7.43	-7.16	0.81	1.86	3.39	4.14
1949	18.71	16.1	23.31	21.04	23.05	23.52	1.12	2.33	6.44	3.31
1950	55.22	31.08	23.11	52.16	32.26	31.01	1.22	0.7	0.05	2.12
1951	14.36	24.78	20.05	12.27	15.74	16.26	1.49	0.36	-3.94	-2.69

Year	F/F Lrg Val Index	F/F Lrg Co. Index	F/F Lrg Gro Index	F/F Sml Val Index	F/F Sml Co. Index	F/F Sml Gro Index	One Month T-Bills	5-Year T Notes	Long Term Gov't Bonds	Long Term Corp. Bonds
1952	19.54	13.34	13.38	8.59	9.46	8.55	1.65	1.63	1.16	3.52
1953	-7.04	0.24	2.29	-6.92	-0.97	-0.68	1.83	3.23	3.63	3.41
1954	77.32	48.13	47.79	63.43	60.77	43.2	0.86	2.7	7.18	5.39
1955	29.78	18.85	28.5	23.47	20.95	13.95	1.57	-0.66	-1.28	0.48
1956	3.37	12.97	6.52	5.98	7.21	7.65	2.47	-0.42	-5.58	-6.81
1957	-22.72	-8.23	-9.14	-15.9	-14.52	-16.99	3.15	7.84	7.47	8.71
1958	72.3	45.34	41.62	69.67	57.18	75.22	1.53	-1.3	-6.11	-2.22
1959	18.82	9.66	13.15	17.42	19.72	21.42	2.97	-0.38	-2.28	-0.97
1960	-8.56	8.57	-2.36	-6.02	-1.78	-1.78	2.67	11.75	13.79	9.07
1961	28.89	26.73	26.43	30.85	30.27	22.2	2.12	1.87	0.96	4.82
1962	-3.09	-5.46	-10.89	-9.47	-15.37	-22.33	2.72	5.58	6.88	7.95
1963	32.35	17.07	21.88	28.34	16.72	7.98	3.11	1.64	1.21	2.19
1964	19.16	20.28	14.48	22.9	17.54	8.13	3.53	4.03	3.51	4.77
1965	22.42	10.08	13.36	42.5	31.84	39.99	3.92	1.01	0.7	-0.46
1966	-10.21	-6.11	-10.77	-7.76	-5.67	-5.32	4.75	4.68	3.65	0.2
1967	31.74	15.92	29.17	67.55	72.71	88.42	4.2	1	-9.19	-4.95
1968	27.08	15.86	4.03	45.81	41.11	32.73	5.22	4.53	-0.26	2.57
1969	-16.39	-16.75	2.88	-25.84	-22.71	-23.68	6.57	-0.74	-5.07	-8.09
1970	10.63	8.12	-5.65	6.62	-7.7	-20.25	6.52	16.85	12.1	18.37
1971	12.55	6.15	23.94	14.47	21.1	25.86	4.39	8.74	13.24	11.01
1972	18.62	11.21	21.32	7.28	6.76	0.39	3.84	5.17	5.67	7.26
1973	-3.67	-8.66	-21.79	-27.23	-33.62	-45.07	6.93	4.61	-1.1	1.14
1974	-23.4	-22.95	-29.24	-19.02	-26.49	-31.9	8.01	5.68	4.35	-3.06
1975	55.9	41.92	34.44	57.12	58.94	61.32	5.8	7.82	9.19	14.64
1976	44.62	41.01	17.54	59.13	47.23	38.2	5.08	12.88	16.76	18.65
1977	1.64	-0.76	-9.46	23.82	17.96	19.35	5.13	1.4	-0.65	1.71
1978	3.48	6.73	7	22.12	19.93	17.65	7.2	3.49	-1.18	-0.07
1979	22.67	23.39	16.59	38.33	36.69	48.84	10.38	4.1	-1.21	-4.19
1980	16.45	37.54	35.2	22.28	31	52.66	11.26	3.9	-3.96	-2.61
1981	12.8	-7.62	-7.13	17.68	13.8	-11.53	14.72	9.44	1.86	-0.96
1982	27.67	17.41	21.48	39.86	33.35	19.72	10.53	29.1	40.37	43.79
1983	26.92	24.97	14.67	47.58	38.69	22.12	8.8	7.41	0.69	4.7
1984	16.17	5.67	-0.72	7.52	0.6	-12.84	9.78	14.03	15.54	16.39
1985	31.75	32.01	32.64	32.12	32.61	28.91	7.73	20.34	30.96	30.9
1986	21.82	20.65	14.38	14.5	10.41	1.95	6.15	15.13	24.45	19.85
1987	-2.76	3.25	7.43	-7.12	-3.88	-12.24	5.46	2.9	-2.7	-0.27

Year	F/F Lrg Val Index	F/F Lrg Co. Index	F/F Lrg Gro Index	F/F Sml Val Index	F/F Sml Co. Index	F/F Sml Gro Index	One Month T-Bills	5-Year T Notes	Long Term Gov't Bonds	Long Term Corp. Bonds
1988	25.96	17.53	12.53	30.76	28.78	16.63	6.36	6.09	9.68	10.7
1989	29.7	24.63	36.11	15.7	18.13	20.58	8.38	13.27	18.1	16.23
1990	-12.75	-5.62	1.06	-25.13	-17.65	-17.74	7.82	9.74	6.2	6.78
1991	27.35	22.14	43.33	40.56	47.04	54.73	5.6	15.31	19.26	19.89
1992	23.57	9.65	6.41	34.76	22.4	5.82	3.5	7.2	9.41	9.39
1993	19.51	16.13	2.38	29.41	18.41	12.64	2.9	11.24	18.24	13.19
1994	-5.78	0.09	1.95	3.21	-1.41	-4.36	3.91	-5.13	-7.78	-7.03
1995	37.68	36.74	37.16	27.69	27.95	35.13	5.6	16.11	31.67	26.39
1996	13.35	26.3	21.25	20.71	22.24	12.36	5.2	2.09	-0.92	1.4
1997	31.88	32.28	31.61	37.29	32.01	15.29	5.25	8.38	15.87	12.95
1998	16.23	9.23	34.64	-8.63	-4.19	3.04	4.85	10.22	13.07	10.76
1999	-0.22	7.51	29.43	5.59	11.37	54.75	4.69	-1.76	-8.99	-7.45
2000	5.8	4.62	-13.63	-0.8	4.67	-24.15	5.88	12.6	21.49	12.85
2001	-1.18	-1.85	-15.59	40.24	26.2	0.16	3.85	7.61	3.7	10.65
2002	-32.53	-15.89	-21.5	-12.41	-13.57	-30.87	1.63	12.95	17.84	16.33
2003	35.07	33.85	26.29	74.69	51.56	53.2	1.02	2.4	1.44	5.27

Data Source: Dimensional Fund Advisors. F/F is Fama/French.
Eugene Fama University of Chicago; Kenneth French MIT.

G

Glossary

1:1 – the idea (actually a truism), expressed as a ratio, that a portfolio invested in the entire equity market will achieve a return that is equal to the total market with a probability of 100 percent – a 1 out of 1 chance. Actual portfolios can only approximate a total market portfolio and, consequently, may not achieve returns exactly equal to market return. The goal, however, is to earn market return as close to 1:1 as possible.

Active management – the system of investment management that is dependent on successfully predicting market and security movements (timing) and security selection (picking).

Active marketing – the marketing by the financial services establishment which tends to promote emotional decisions by consumers.

Cost of life – total living expenses individuals must cover with either their current incomes if they are still working or their pensions, government programs or portfolio investments if they are retired.

Direct pay – money paid exclusively from a client, directly to an advisory firm for financial advice. Direct pay is different from the entrenched Wall Street system of indirect payments, subsidies and sales commissions.

Efficient analyst paradox – logical conclusion that the work of many highly skilled securities analysts will ensure efficient market prices, thus making those same skilled analysts unable to consistently find undervalued stocks.

Extended market – the exposure afforded by the additional securities present in a *market return* strategy above and beyond normal portfolio composition. (The MRP™ may hold as many as 15,000 to 16,000 individual securities.)

Facilitators – representatives from the financial services industry who offer products that tend to appeal to investor emotions rather than investor needs.

Fiduciary – advisors who act in the best interests of their client and disclose any real or implied conflicts of interest. This is generally a higher standard than is customary in the financial services industry.

Giant Portfolio Stop-Loss effect – beneficial effect caused by the super-diversification found in a Market Return Portfolio™, which tends to limit volatility during down markets.

Independent advisor – advisor who is not employed or related in any way to brokerage houses, banks or other financial institutions that may profit from offering incentives to advisors for recommending particular products. An independent advisor will be associated with a fee-based registered investment advisor (RIA).

Institutional asset class funds – low cost no-load mutual funds designed to represent whole asset classes as defined by Modern Portfolio Theory. Characteristically, they maintain their asset class integrity so that diversification remains dependable. These funds are used by large institutional investors (such as pension and scholarship funds) and by the clients of many independent advisors.

Market return – nothing more, nothing less than the return readily available when investors efficiently harness the power of capital markets.

Market Return Portfolio™ – a portfolio that is constructed with the objective of earning market return by using low cost, no-load institutional asset class mutual funds.

Misaligned interests – financial interests of the investor that are in conflict with the financial interests of the institutions and representatives who provide advice and investment products.

Modern Portfolio Theory (MPT) – research in finance over the last 50+ years that relates to the risk and return characteristics of various asset classes when they are combined to create investment portfolios.

Academicians such as Harry Markowitz, William Sharpe, Merton Miller, Franco Modigliani and Eugene Fama are some of the major contributors to this field of research.

Proprietary products – products designed and managed by institutions whose representatives then recommend them to investors. Proprietary products often have higher costs and steep penalties for selling, which keep investors tied to the products.

Super-diversification –high degree of diversification that occurs when institutional asset class funds are used to construct a portfolio. IACFs provide broad and deep representation of the capital markets.

There for the taking – idea that market return is accessible to all investors in a free capital market system.

Reading List

There for the Taking was written for the general reader who may have limited knowledge about the world of finance. We purposefully kept to the central key points that could change a reader's paradigm about investing and left out most discussions of the research and data. If you now have a newfound interest in investing or Modern Portfolio Theory then you should explore some of the books on the list below.

1. *A Random Walk Down Wall Street*, Burton Malkiel. W.W. Norton & Company, New York, 1996.

2. *Against the Gods*, Peter L. Bernstein. John Wiley & Sons, Inc., New York, 1998.

3. *Bogle on Mutual Funds*, John Bogle. McGraw-Hill, New York, 1993.

4. *Does Your Broker Owe You Money?*, Daniel R. Solin. Alpha Books, Indianapolis, 2003.

5. *Investment Policy, How to Win the Losers Game*, Charles Ellis. Irwin Professional Publishing, Chicago, 1993.

6. *Promises to Keep, Saving Social Security's Dream*, Marshall N. Carter and William G. Shipman. Regnery Publishing, Inc., Washington, D.C., 1996

7. *Take on The Street*, Arthur Levitt. Pantheon Books, New York, 2002.

8. *The Coming Generational Storm*, Laurence J. Kotlikoff and Scott Burns. The MIT Press, Cambridge, Massachusetts, 2004.

9. *The Four Pillars of Investing*, William Bernstein. McGraw-Hill, New York, 2002.

10. *The Prudent Investor's Guide to Beating Wall Street at Its Own Game*, John J. Bowen & Daniel C. Goldie. McGraw-Hill, New York, 1998.

11. *The Unbeatable Market*, Ron Ross. Bookmasters, Inc., Mansfield, Ohio, 2002.

12. *Why Smart People Make Big Money Mistakes and How to Correct Them*, Gary Belsky and Thomas Gilovich. Simon & Schuster, New York, 1999.

A
Acknowledgments

Sir Winston Churchill once said, "Writing a book is an adventure: it begins as an amusement, then it becomes a mistress, then a master, and finally a tyrant."

Truer words were never spoken.

Appreciation is first due to all the brilliant economic thinkers that have paved the way for those of us who now declare their wisdom. Work from men such as Friedrich Hayek, Harry Markowitz, William Sharpe and Eugene Fama have forever changed our understanding of capital markets for the better. Also, many thanks to the professionals at Dimensional Fund Advisors for their vast wealth of information, their creativity and innovation and their willingness to share their wisdom with independent advisors and individual investors.

I am also grateful to investment pioneers like John Bogle and members of the media such as Jonathan Clements of the *Wall Street Journal* and syndicated columnist Scott Burns who are truly taking a stand for individual investors with their good work.

A project to compile thoughts and information in a way that can be communicated logically and effectively is an enormous task. It would never have been accomplished without the hard work and dedication of my staff. Thank you Matt Sanders, Joy Justice, Rachel Nolte and Becky Holt. You all deserve to have your names on the front cover. Thank you to Sharon Feagin for your help all these years. We've come a long way together. Thanks also to Cristina and Claire Alston for letting me use your husband/daddy on so many weekends. Lance, your insight, suggestions, and contributions to the book have been outstanding. I am fortunate to have such a good business partner.

Thanks to all the proofreaders that improved this book immeasurably with their thoughtful suggestions. In particular, Gary Belsky, Daniel Solin, Larry and Janie Trantham, Tom Westerfield, Ellen Bruno, Bob Irish and Don Wass. Your interest in our efforts was both flattering and humbling.

A special thanks to Alex Booras whose guidance and enthusiasm cannot be replaced. You have brightened our days as we worked extra hours, and your sensible approach has been a key to our success.

Thanks to the Synerjet team of Jet Parker and Nick Loyless for helping us with the numerous details and to Suzanne Miller for leading us through the complexities of the book business.

Thanks to our editor, Cindie Geddes, for bringing to remembrance all those wonderful rules of the English language that we thought we could discard once the exam was completed. You gently corrected without distorting the message. You are an able craftsman.

Thanks to my good friends and brothers Brent Smith, Oran Cogdill, Felix Chambers, and Randy Little for your humor, competitive challenges, your example and most of all your camaraderie. Also many thanks to Charlie Classe and Gary Simpson for your friendship and professional guidance and to Norris Hodgin for recommending me so many years ago.

I want to offer a heartfelt thank you to our clients. Without you, there is no career, no profession, and no book. Your loyalty and relationships are what make our professional lives so fulfilling.

Thanks to the love of my life, Elizabeth, and my sons Johnathan and Daniel. You sacrificed during the unusually long hours as I engaged in a project you knew I was passionate about. You may now have me back.

I want to say thank you to my in-laws, Dr. Jess and Packy Bescos who I have come to love and appreciate more each year. Thanks again for entrusting me with your precious daughter two decades ago.

Finally, thanks to Lawrence and Mary Whiddon. You raised me right and taught me many valuable lessons in both word and deed; among them this one: "That man is the wealthiest whose satisfactions are the simplest."

James N. Whiddon

Index

Galilei, Galileo, 79
Great Depression, 15, 89, 91, 95
Greenspan, Alan, 24, 25, 127
Growth asset classes, 115
Growth stocks, 115, 122
Hindsight bias, 16, 119
Holmes, Oliver Wendall, 126
IAR, 71, 72
Independent, 71, 72, 73, 75, 106, 111, 122, 152, 157
Indexers, 110
Individual stocks, 45, 105
Inflation, 27, 55, 82, 83, 85, 89, 103
institutional asset class funds (IACFs), 106
International markets, 115
International stocks, 90, 107, 136
Investing, 7, 8, 9, 10, 11, 16, 19, 21, 23, 24, 27, 31, 34, 44, 51, 53, 55, 56, 60, 69, 70, 71, 81, 86, 105, 115, 116, 155
Investment Advisory Representative (IAR), 71
IPS, 24, 64, 123
Iraqi Freedom, 87
Japan, 25, 115, 138, 142, 143, 144
Kennedy, 89
Keynes, John Maynard, 26
long-term, iii, 10, 19, 24, 27, 28, 39, 42, 56, 60, 62, 64, 70, 82, 84, 85, 86, 90, 91, 108, 112, 115, 120, 123
long-term capital gains, 108
management fees, 107
marginal tax rates, 83
market return, 10, 11, 31, 33, 34, 37, 44, 45, 46, 51, 54, 65, 77, 81, 82, 86, 90, 91, 92, 93, 94, 95, 97, 100, 102, 106, 109, 110, 112, 117, 118, 119, 122, 123, 125, 151, 152, 153
market return strategy, 46, 100, 102, 125, 151
market risk, 39, 94, 102, 126, 135
market timing, 9, 15, 17, 20, 21, 24, 26, 28, 29, 34, 39, 56
misaligned interests, 47, 57, 66, 69, 70, 109
Morningstar, 38, 57, 58, 59, 62, 92, 94, 96, 97, 98, 99, 127, 129, 130, 132, 134
MPT, 106, 152

MSCI EAFE, 110, 131, 132, 136, 137, 139, 144, 145
mutual fund expense ratios, 47, 62
NASD, 68
National Association of Securities Dealers (NASD), 68
National Bureau of Economic Research (NBER), 40
NBER, 40
no losers, 7
no-load funds, 107
objectivity, 69, 71, 72
operating expenses, 107
Paine, Thomas, 13
Pearl Harbor, 89
picking, 9, 10, 31, 34, 36, 39, 41, 43, 44, 46, 48, 50, 53, 54, 57, 58, 60, 62, 63, 64, 65, 66, 92, 107, 119, 123, 151
portfolio, 9, 11, 15, 24, 31, 34, 39, 40, 41, 48, 50, 53, 54, 60, 61, 64, 65, 70, 83, 84, 86, 87, 92, 93, 95, 97, 100, 103, 105, 106, 107, 108, 109, 110, 112, 113, 114, 115, 117, 119, 120, 122, 129, 132, 134, 135, 136, 139, 141, 143, 151, 152, 153
portfolio filter, 108
portfolio protection, 86
pre-retirement, 85
protection, 29, 86, 95, 96, 97, 98, 102
purchasing power, 29, 82, 86, 102
random, 17, 19, 21, 50, 56, 58, 65
randomness, 29
Reagan, Ronald, 31
real rate of return, 83
referrals, 74
Registered Investment Advisor, 71, 72
REIT, 114
retiree, 121
retirement, 15, 24, 74, 84, 85, 110, 118, 122
returns, iii, 9, 10, 11, 23, 31, 33, 37, 43, 44, 51, 53, 55, 56, 59, 60, 62, 63, 64, 66, 86, 87, 89, 91, 92, 93, 97, 100, 106, 110, 122, 126, 134, 135, 137, 138, 139, 144, 151

NOTES